THE GAME & FISH MASTERY LIBRARY

STICKS & STONES

The Art of Grilling on Plank, Vine and Stone

By Ted Reader and Kathleen Sloan

WILLOW CREEK PRESS

Minocqua, Wisconsin

A Denise Schon Book

A Denise Schon Book

Published by: Willow Creek Press, P.O. Box 147, Minocqua, Wisconsin
For information on other Willow Creek titles, call 1-800-850-9453

Library of Congress Cataloging-in-Publication Data
Reader, Ted.
    Sticks & stones : the art of grilling on plank, vine, and stone /
by Ted Reader and Kathleen Sloan.
      p. cm. – (The game & fish mastery library)
ISBN: 1-57223-221-8
1. Barbecue cookery. I. Sloan, Kathleen. II. Title. III. Title: Sticks and stones. IV. Series.
TX840.B3R43   1999
641.5'784–dc21

                                                           99-18070
                                                             CIP

Produced by: Denise Schon Books Inc.
Design: Dianne Eastman
Editor: Kirsten Hanson
Index: Barbara Schon

Published in Canada by Macmillan Canada, CDG Books Canada, Inc. Toronto, Canada
Printed and bound in Canada by Friesens, Altona, Manitoba, Canada
Printed on acid-free paper

1 2 3 4 5   FP   03 02 01 00 99

Years ago I learned to prepare cedar-planked salmon; I featured it on Cottage Country Television, and shared my recipe with President's Choice. It was a hit, and I have been planking ever since.

To my good friend Kathleen Sloan, who has endured many hours of recipe testing, thanks for her exceptional palette and her way with words. To my wonderful family for all their love and support. To my friend Chef Luther Miller for his talent and skill in testing these recipes.

Lastly, to my love Pamela, you have given me love and encouragement in all that I do. Thank you for loving me and for being my best critic.

Savor the flavor of smoke,

Chef Ted Reader

From the moment I tasted my first cedar-planked salmon I was hooked on the method of plank-grilling, so when my friend Chef Ted Reader suggested that we should produce a cookbook on the subject, he was already preaching to the converted. I am pleased and proud to be part of this endeavor and am indebted to Ted for making me part of it.

A big thank-you goes to Denise Schon and everyone at Denise Schon Books for their collective and invaluable help and shared enthusiasm. My thanks also go to Dianne Eastman, Jennifer McLagan and Andreas Trauttmansdorff for their creative skill in bringing beauty and style to this contemporary collection of recipes and the ancient cooking methods that inspired them.

Kathleen Sloan

Contents

Introduction 6

CHAPTER 1

In the Beginning 12

SOUPS AND STARTERS

CHAPTER 2

From the Land 32

CHICKEN, BEEF, PORK, LAMB, TURKEY, GAME

CHAPTER 3

From the Sea 50

FISH AND SEAFOOD

CHAPTER 4

From the Earth 72

SIDES AND SAUCES

CHAPTER 5

From the Orchard 84

SWEETS AND TREATS

Introduction

This book respectfully takes its inspiration from the Pacific Northwest Native art of plank-grilling, an ancient tradition of cooking sides of fresh fish — specifically salmon — on alderwood or cedar. The classic technique involved splitting open a salmon, binding it to a piece of driftwood, and cooking it vertically downwind of a roaring open fire. Thought by many to be the forerunner of today's barbecue, this method is the essence of cooking at its most primal, using natural elements to create food imbued with flavor, touched by fire and licked with smoke. The Native peoples also developed hot-stone cooking — heating solid, flat rocks in a fire and fashioning an earth and stone pit oven in which to sear fresh fish and seafood.

As the food cooks, almost basting itself in its own oils and juices, it absorbs fragrant wood smoke.

Sticks and Stones celebrates these elemental culinary art forms in a thoroughly contemporary way, using aromatic woods, vines and terra-cotta or granite pieces to reunite — albeit in a modern fashion — the traditional Native influences of wood, stone, sea and smoke.

We like to think of the methods described in this book as a natural evolution of an original rudimentary cooking style. Plank-grilling fish and other foods on sections of soaked aromatic woods set over a grill is surely one of the most sensual culinary experiences. As the food cooks, almost basting itself in its own oils and juices, it absorbs fragrant wood smoke to achieve a layering of flavors not found in any other form of cooking.

We've also included information and recipes using fragrant, aromatic vine cuttings and herb and spice branches — a concept that, while perhaps not part of Native North American traditions, might whimsically be thought of as the "applied theory."

GETTING STARTED

BUYING PLANKS

Use whatever untreated, aromatic wood you prefer (or can readily obtain) for any of the recipes. We do not recommend using Eastern cedar, pine, poplar, or birch. Unless you live on the edge of a forest, you'll probably source your cooking planks at a local lumberyard or building supply outlet. Make sure to specify construction grade, untreated wood, no more than 1 inch thick (5/8 inch is best), 8 to 10 inches wide and 10 to 12 inches long. Although we suggest a specific wood for each recipe (varieties such as cedar, maple, oak, hickory, alderwood, peachwood and applewood), the recipes may be reproduced using any of these woods. Feel free to adopt a mix-and-match approach. Just make sure the wood is untreated in any way. When buying cedar or other woods for planking, ask the store to cut the wood into 10- to 12-inch lengths. You may wish to purchase several pieces at once — when you become accustomed to this method of grilling, you'll want to do it often.

WHERE THERE'S SMOKE ... THERE'S FLAVOR

Anyone who is planning to plank-grill must be prepared for the amount of smoke that is generated. This aromatic smoke, naturally produced when a water-soaked plank is set over a hot grill, imbues the food with a characteristically intense wood flavor. When you grill on wood planks you are in effect cooking with aromatic smoke.

You must exercise caution when lifting the grill lid to baste or check food because planking produces a great deal more smoke than conventional grilling. Be aware too, that opening the grill lid too often will lower the temperature, thereby increasing the cooking time.

This book also includes planking recipes using a conventional oven. The plank sits in a roasting pan which is partially filled with water, juice or apple cider and preheated in a very hot oven. When you plank-bake in this way you are in effect cooking with aromatic steam. This method works so well — providing flavor through the wood steam and retaining valuable meat juices — that you may never prepare conventional roasts again.

CAN I REUSE MY PLANKS?

If the planks are not too badly charred from the grill, you may be able to reuse them once. Planks that have been used in the oven, however, can often be reused two or three times.

SOAKING PLANKS

We cannot overemphasize the vital importance of presoaking the planks for plank-grilling – you simply can't plank-grill with dry wood. On an outdoor grill, dry planks can ignite fully. We recommend soaking wood for about six hours. Even if you are short of time, soak the wood for at least one hour before planking. *When we designate a "soaked plank" at the beginning of each recipe we are referring to either of these lengths of time.* We often soak planks overnight weighed down with heavy cans or stones to completely submerge the wood in water.

Presoaking is generally not necessary for oven-planking, since the wood is usually submerged in a liquid in a roasting pan. However, you must be careful to monitor the level of liquid and add more water or juice as necessary (usually every 15 minutes or so) to keep the plank and the pan from burning. There are a few oven recipes here that call for presoaked planks; in these cases the planks are not submerged in liquid in the oven.

USING STONES

The rule of thumb for cooking with stone is never to use porous rocks (such as shale). Porous rocks can retain water and may explode when heated to a high temperature. Look for solid, completely dry, relatively flat stones with no cracks. Rocks that are slightly damp or cracked can also explode dangerously. We do not recommend gathering rocks at the seaside. While we specify readily available slabs of granite or marble for our "stone" recipes, you may use larger solid pieces of these rocks instead. A thicker rock may take longer to preheat than a 1-inch slab of granite or marble.

Why use stones? Because for some foods, such as scallops, oysters, fish fillets and pizza, you want a surface that doesn't impart flavor and cooks very fast. Look for pieces of stone – terra-cotta, marble, or granite – at building supply outlets. You can also buy ceramic pizza stones at kitchenware outlets. You may even have a suitable piece of stone or terra-cotta left over from renovating a kitchen or bathroom. Choose pieces about the same dimensions as wood planks. Obviously you will be able to reuse them for quite a while.

For centuries, French wine producers have added their fall cuttings to cooking fires, because the vines impart a subtle sweet, smoky flavor to foods. Inspired by this, we use vine cuttings (available at specialty food shops and kitchenware outlets) to skewer pieces of meat, seafood or vegetables for grilling. Wooden skewers, soaked in wine, cider, bourbon, sherry or port can also be used to great effect, as can stripped rosemary branches, lemon grass, slender cinnamon sticks or whittled licorice root. You'll also find recipes in this book for grilling foods wrapped in leaves. Try thoroughly washed, large green maple leaves if available, or grape or banana leaves (often available at Latin American markets). You can be quite creative in this style of cooking with wonderful results. For example, a soaked birch-bark wrapping (a traditional technique of the Australian Aboriginal peoples) will give bread, oysters, trout, scallops and chicken a smoky mushroom flavor.

Vines, when used as skewers, impart a subtle sweet, smoky flavor to foods.

SAFETY PRECAUTIONS

When cooking on plank and stone, use all of your senses — especially your common sense. Your nose and ears will tell you when the plank is ready. Once you hear the wood begin to crackle and smell the woodsmoke (generally three to five minutes after placing the plank on the grill) you'll know it's time to get plank-grilling. It is very important to keep a full spray bottle of water at hand when planking, and use it to extinguish flames as they creep round the edge of the hot plank. While we don't mean to suggest you'll set the deck on fire, you may want to invest in a portable fire extinguisher, which is a sensible addition to every home anyway. It is also a good idea to have a bucket of water handy beside the grill. Use it to plunge the used plank in after you've removed the cooked food from it, if the plank is too badly charred to use again. There is no need to oil planks, although in some recipes coarse sea salt is used to draw more of the aromatics out of the wood.

FIRED UP

We strongly recommend that you use a gas grill for these recipes because it will generate the constant level of high heat necessary for plank-grilling. Obviously you can use a charcoal grill, or even a safely made beachside fire, but you must build a good strong fire and maintain it with extra charcoal or hardwood as needed. Planking requires a strong and constant heat for the entire duration of the cooking time in order to sufficiently heat the wood and thereby cook the food.

THE SPIRIT OF THE BOOK

In the following pages you'll find more than 50 thoroughly contemporary recipes organized in chapters devoted to soups, salads, appetizers, main meat and seafood courses, side dishes, sauces and even imaginative desserts such as *Maple-Planked Bourbon-Soaked Peach Melba with Warm Summer Berries and Sour Cream Ice* – simply outstanding.

After you familiarize yourself with the basic method (which won't take long), you will likely begin to invent your own original plank-grilled preparations.

Sticks and Stones is a modern guide to an ancient method of cooking. We hope you enjoy both our book and the culinary genre in the spirit with which they were conceived – to provide sustenance and pleasure.

CHAPTER 1

In the Beginning

SOUPS AND STARTERS

Wood-Smoked Butternut Squash Soup
with Cumin-Roasted Pearl Onions

Planked Cheddar and Brown Ale Soup

Mesquite-Smoked Corn Chowder
with Spicy Sausage

Granite-Roasted Prosciutto-Wrapped Figs
Stuffed with Cambazola

Cedar-Roasted Shallot and Shiitake Polenta

Terra-Cotta Pizza with Caramelized Onion,
Bacon and Gorgonzola

Terra-Cotta-Roasted Mussels and Clams
with Riesling Dill Butter Sauce

Chardonnay-Vine-Skewered Shrimp
and Pineapple with Chile Lime Rub

Maple-Planked Brie with Roasted Garlic
and Peppers

Cedar-Planked Onion and
Portobello Mushroom Focaccia

Plank-Smoked Garlic Risotto
with Taleggio and Peas

Newfoundland Cod Cakes on the Rocks
with Bonavista Tartar Sauce

Black-Peppered Quail on Cinnamon Sticks
with Wheat Berry and Smoked-Bacon Salad

This chapter demonstrates just how versatile the art of plank-grilling can be. Here you'll find recipes for rich, smoke-imbued soups and wonderfully inventive appetizers, all of which have touched plank or stone in some form or other.

When central components, such as the butternut squash for the *Wood-Smoked Butternut Squash Soup with Cumin-Roasted Pearl Onions,* are planked, the whole dish takes on the smoke and flavor of the wood. We have chosen ingredients that have the sturdiness and natural ability to stand up to the rigors and high heat of planking: vegetables such as onions, squash, red peppers, and corn, hefty portobello mushrooms, and big cheeses such as Cheddar (wrapped tightly in wide, green leaves before planking).

Use the starters in this chapter to whet appetites and to introduce the uninitiated to these intense flavors. Some starters will make great light meals on their own, especially paired with one of the soups — try the *Planked Cheddar and Brown Ale Soup* with *Cedar-Planked Onion and Portobello Mushroom Focaccia.* Many people choose two starters when they dine out these days, which is why we have created first courses that are a little more substantial than the average appetizer: *Plank-Smoked Garlic Risotto with Taleggio and Peas* and *Newfoundland Cod Cakes on the Rocks with Bonavista Tartar Sauce* make great dining companions.

In this chapter we also include a recipe for *Bone Dust Barbecue Spice.* We strongly suggest you make a batch of this wonderful all-round grilling spice rub at the outset since it shows up in many recipes throughout this book.

Wood-Smoked Butternut Squash Soup with Cumin-Roasted Pearl Onions

Squash takes on an entirely new dimension when planked. In this case, the result is a beautiful, smoky-sweet flavored soup perfect for fall entertaining. Make the Cumin-Roasted Pearl Onions ahead of time, if you wish, and warm them slightly before adding to the soup. In place of butternut squash, you might substitute small sugar pumpkins or acorn squash. Soak the planks for at least an hour and preferably 6 hours, or overnight.

SERVES 8

2 planks such as cedar or maple, soaked
2 tbsp olive oil
6 cloves garlic, roughly chopped
1 large onion, sliced
1 large butternut squash, peeled, seeded and cut into 1-inch strips
2 potatoes, peeled and diced
1 tbsp chopped fresh thyme
3 cups fresh orange juice
6 cups chicken or vegetable broth
2 tsp *Bone Dust Barbecue Spice* (recipe follows)
salt and freshly ground pepper
Cumin-Roasted Pearl Onions (recipe follows)

Preheat grill to high.

In large bowl, combine oil, garlic and onions. Season onion mixture and squash with salt and pepper.

Place soaked planks on grill, close lid and bake for 3 to 5 minutes until the planks begin to crackle and smoke. Carefully lift lid, and place sliced onion and squash on planks. Close lid and plank-bake for 45 minutes. From time to time, turn vegetables and check to make sure the wood is not burning. If necessary, use spray bottle to extinguish any flames, reduce heat to medium and continue to cook until vegetables are tender.

Remove plank from grill and transfer smoked onions to large, heavy soup pot. Sauté for 2 minutes over medium-high heat. Add squash and diced potatoes and sauté for 3 minutes. Add thyme, orange juice, chicken broth and *Bone Dust*. Bring to a boil, reduce heat to medium-low and let simmer for 30 to 45 minutes, stirring occasionally. Purée the mixture with hand blender (or in blender or food processor) until smooth. Pour through sieve, rubbing vegetables against sides to extract as much liquid as possible. Wipe large pot clean and return soup to it. Heat through over medium heat. Adjust seasoning with salt and pepper. Garnish with *Cumin-Roasted Pearl Onions*.

Cumin-Roasted Pearl Onions

To remove onion skins, parboil the onions for just a few minutes, then plunge them into cold water – the skins should rub off quite easily.

2 cups pearl onions
    (if frozen, thaw before using)
2 tbsp olive oil

2 cloves garlic, finely chopped
1-1/2 tsp ground cumin
salt and freshly ground pepper

Preheat oven to 400°F.

In mixing bowl, toss together onions, olive oil, garlic and ground cumin. Season with salt and pepper. Place onion mixture in shallow ovenproof dish and roast in oven for 30 to 40 minutes, stirring occasionally, until onions are uniformly golden brown and slightly crisp.

Bone Dust Barbecue Spice

Perhaps we should call this our "Soon-to-Be-Famous" Bone Dust Barbecue Spice. This recipe makes quite a bit, which is just as well, since you will see Bone Dust listed as an ingredient in many of the recipes in this book. It is an invaluable pantry staple – great for rubbing into just about anything you plank, grill or roast. If using whole spices, use an electric coffee mill or a mortar and pestle to grind spices to a powder.

MAKES APPROXIMATELY 2-1/2 CUPS

1/2 cup paprika
1/4 cup chili powder
3 tbsp salt
2 tbsp ground coriander
2 tbsp garlic powder
2 tbsp white sugar
2 tbsp curry powder

2 tbsp dry hot mustard
1 tbsp freshly ground black pepper
1 tbsp ground basil
1 tbsp ground thyme
1 tbsp ground cumin
1 tbsp cayenne

In bowl, mix all ingredients together well. Store in tightly sealed container.

Planked Cheddar and Brown Ale Soup

Grilled cheese takes on a whole other dimension! This intensely flavorful and quite magnificent soup is perfect for a frigid winter day, and it makes a wonderful precursor to Maple-Planked Prime Rib Roast *(page 37). You can substitute banana or grape leaves for the maple leaves.*

SERVES 6 TO 8

1 maple plank, soaked
12 large green maple leaves
1 lb block white Cheddar cheese
  (aged at least 2 years)
2 tbsp *Bone Dust Barbecue Spice*
  (page 15)
1 large Spanish onion, sliced
6 cloves garlic, peeled
3 bottles (12 fl oz each) dark ale
1/4 cup butter

2 large leeks, rinsed, trimmed
  and thinly sliced
1/4 cup all-purpose flour
6–8 cups chicken broth
2 medium Yukon Gold potatoes,
  peeled and diced
2 tbsp chopped fresh thyme
1/2 cup whipping cream
salt and freshly ground pepper
homemade or store-bought croutons

Soak leaves in water for 5 minutes. Drain and shake off excess water. Season cheese with *Bone Dust* making sure to rub mixture well into cheese. Tightly wrap cheese in leaves and secure with toothpicks or string.

Preheat grill to high. Place soaked plank on grill and heat until crackling. Place wrapped cheese in center of plank and arrange sliced onions and garlic cloves over and around cheese. Close lid and plank-bake for 12 to 15 minutes, checking occasionally to make sure cheese is not escaping from its leaf wrapping.

Remove plank from grill. Carefully unwrap cheese and transfer to a bowl with char-smoked onions and garlic. Cover and place in a warm oven while you prepare soup.

Pour 2 bottles of ale into a large, heavy saucepan. Bring to boil then reduce heat to medium-low. Let beer gently boil for about 30 minutes, until reduced to a thick syrup. Remove from heat and set aside.

In large, heavy soup pot, melt butter over medium-high heat. Add leeks and sauté for 3 to 5 minutes until leeks are transparent and tender. Add flour and stir for another 2 to 3 minutes. Do not brown flour. Whisking constantly, slowly add remaining bottle of ale. Add chicken broth, 1 cup at a time, whisking to discourage lumping. When all chicken broth has been incorporated, add potatoes and thyme. Bring to rolling boil, reduce heat and let soup simmer for 30 minutes or until potatoes are tender. Add cheese, onions and garlic. Purée mixture with hand blender (or in blender or food processor). Add cream and season with salt and pepper to taste. Garnish each serving with a drizzle of the ale reduction and croutons.

Mesquite-Smoked Corn Chowder with Spicy Sausage

Reserve this sturdy, big-flavored chowder – almost a meal in itself – for the close of summer when fresh corn is plentiful. Plank more corn than you need then pack the shaved kernels in resealable freezer bags so you can make this soup again when fresh corn season is long past. With the plank-roasting method, we shuck the ears of corn to allow the aromatic flavors of the wood to penetrate the kernels.

SERVES 8 TO 12

2 mesquite or hickory planks, soaked

2 Spanish onions, sliced

3 cloves garlic, chopped

1 tbsp *Bone Dust Barbecue Spice*
   (page 15)

2 tbsp olive oil

6 ears peaches-and-cream corn, shucked

3 fresh, spicy sausages (12–16 oz total)

2 tbsp butter

2 large Yukon Gold potatoes,
   peeled and diced

6 cups chicken or vegetable broth

1 cup whipping cream

1 tbsp chopped fresh sage

salt and freshly ground pepper

Preheat grill to high.

In large bowl, combine onions, garlic, *Bone Dust* and olive oil.

Place soaked planks onto preheated grill and bake for 3 to 5 minutes until they begin to crackle and smoke. Place corn on one plank and sausages on the other. Distribute onion mixture over sausages. Close grill lid and plank-bake for 20 to 25 minutes, until sausage is cooked. Check from time to time to make sure that wood has not ignited. If necessary, use spray bottle to extinguish any flames and reduce heat to medium.

Remove plank from grill. Using sharp knife, remove kernels of corn from cobs and reserve. Chop planked onions and reserve. Dice sausages and reserve for garnish.

In a large soup pot, melt butter over medium-high heat. Add chopped onions and sauté for 3 to 5 minutes. Add potatoes and continue to cook for 2 more minutes, stirring constantly. Add chicken broth, bring to a boil, reduce heat and simmer for 20 minutes or until potatoes are tender. Add corn, whipping cream and sage. Season to taste. Heat through briefly and serve garnished with diced sausage.

Granite-Roasted Prosciutto-Wrapped Figs Stuffed with Cambazola

The natural sweetness of fresh figs against the pungency of the cheese and the salty prosciutto makes this a memorable first course — "pure passion," says Ted.

SERVES 8

1 piece granite
8 large ripe purple-black mission figs
2 tbsp maple syrup
1/4 lb cambazola cheese
freshly ground black pepper
8 slices prosciutto

Preheat oven to 425°F. Place granite on middle rack of oven and heat for 20 minutes.

Slice stems off figs and cut each fig 3/4 of the way through the center lengthwise. Drizzle a little maple syrup into center of each fig, then fill with 1 tbsp cambazola cheese. Season with black pepper and wrap each fig closed with a slice of prosciutto.

Using tongs, place wrapped figs on preheated granite and bake for 6 to 8 minutes until prosciutto is slightly crisp and cheese is melted. Remove granite from oven. Using metal spatula, carefully transfer figs to serving dish. Serve with crostini and fresh arugula.

Cedar-Roasted Shallot and Shiitake Polenta

You might expect this would be a recipe for planking set polenta. Instead, however, we have chosen to grill the ingredients that go into the polenta itself. The result is a truly delicious dish made up of several complementary flavors and textures.

SERVES 6

1 cedar plank, soaked
water as needed
12 large shiitake mushrooms,
    stemmed, quartered
6 large shallots, peeled and quartered
6 cloves garlic, peeled and halved
2 tbsp olive oil
1 tbsp chopped fresh thyme
1 tbsp red wine vinegar

salt and freshly ground pepper
6 slices double-smoked bacon, diced
3 cups water
1 tsp salt
1 cup cornmeal (quick-cook if you wish)
3–4 oz provolone cheese, grated
2 tbsp Parmesan cheese, grated
salt and freshly ground pepper
sprigs fresh thyme

Preheat oven to 375°F. In roasting pan or ovenproof dish large enough to accommodate it, place plank and add enough water to come up to top of, but not cover, the wood. Bake for 10 to 15 minutes until wood is quite hot.

Meanwhile, in bowl combine shiitake mushrooms, shallots, garlic, olive oil, thyme, vinegar and a little salt and pepper. Mix well, then transfer mixture to hot plank. Bake for 45 minutes or until slightly crisp and tender. Remove from oven and set to one side; keep warm. While mushrooms and onions are planking, sauté bacon in small skillet, until crisp.

Drain and reserve.

Bring water and salt to rolling boil in medium saucepan. Pour cornmeal into water in a steady stream whisking constantly until fully incorporated. Reduce heat to low and continue to stir, switching to wooden spoon, until mixture is slightly thick and fully cooked. (The time will vary from 5 to 20 minutes depending on type of cornmeal used.) Remove from heat and stir in mushroom-shallot mixture, bacon and cheeses. Season with salt and pepper to taste and garnish each serving with fresh thyme.

Terra-Cotta Pizza with Caramelized Onion, Bacon and Gorgonzola

If you have a round or square pizza stone, use it for this recipe. Otherwise use a large piece of terra-cotta.   **SERVES 2 TO 4**

For the pizza dough:
1 cup warm water
1 tsp sugar
1 package active dry yeast
1 tsp salt
2 tbsp olive oil
3-1/2 cups sifted all-purpose flour

For the pizza toppings:
8 slices bacon, diced
1 large Spanish onion, sliced
3 cloves garlic, minced
1 cup crumbled gorgonzola cheese
1 cup chopped fresh thyme
salt and freshly ground pepper

Warm large mixing bowl with hot water. Drain and add 1 cup warm water to bowl. Sprinkle sugar over surface of warm water and stir to dissolve. Sprinkle yeast over surface and stir to dissolve. Place bowl in warm, draft-free place for a few minutes until yeast begins to froth and foam. Stir in salt and olive oil, then add 2 cups of the flour and beat until smooth. Gradually stir in remaining flour and beat until smooth and soft.

Turn dough out onto lightly floured surface and knead until smooth and elastic, about 10 minutes. Place dough in greased bowl, brush top with a little extra olive oil and cover with a cloth. Let dough rise in a warm place until doubled in size, about 45 to 50 minutes.

In the meantime, make pizza toppings. Sauté bacon in large frying pan until crisp. Transfer bacon with slotted spoon to drain on paper towels. Add onion and garlic to drippings in pan and sauté for 10 to 12 minutes stirring frequently until onions and garlic are caramelized. Season to taste. Remove from pan and let cool.

Once dough has doubled in size, punch down and divide in half. Form each half into a ball. Using rolling pin, roll out first ball of dough to a circle about 12 inches in diameter. Repeat with second ball. Season each circle with a little salt and pepper.

Place terra-cotta or pizza stone on middle rack of oven and preheat to 500°F for 10 to 15 minutes. Place first circle of dough on heated stone and bake for 5 minutes until slightly crisp. Pull out oven rack that holds pizza stone from oven and quickly top dough with half of the caramelized onions and garlic, bacon, crumbled gorgonzola and fresh thyme. Slide rack back into oven and bake for 8 to 10 minutes until toppings are hot and cheese is melted. Remove pizza from oven, cut into 8 pieces and serve. Repeat procedure with second batch of dough.

Terra-Cotta-Roasted Mussels and Clams with Riesling Dill Butter Sauce

This splendid first course begs to be served with lots of warm, crusty bread to mop up all the lovely aromatic juices. You will need a terra-cotta casserole with a lid for this preparation; if you have an open terra-cotta dish, just improvise a lid with foil. Prepare the Riesling Dill Butter Sauce *while the mussels and clams are roasting.*

SERVES 4 TO 6

1 lemon, thinly sliced
3 cloves garlic, thinly sliced
1/2 cup chopped fresh dill
1 lb cherrystone clams, scrubbed clean
1 lb mussels, scrubbed clean
 and debearded

2 tbsp coarse sea salt
Riesling Dill Butter Sauce
 (recipe follows)

Preheat oven to 500°F. Line bottom of terra-cotta casserole with sliced lemon, garlic and dill, cover with lid and bake for 10 minutes.

Keep mussels and clams in two separate piles and season with sea salt. Remove casserole from oven, take off lid and pour in clams. (Clams take longer to cook than mussels.)

Cover and roast for 5 to 7 minutes. Remove from oven, add mussels and roast for 10 more minutes or until all clams and mussels have opened. Discard any that have not opened. Pour *Riesling Dill Butter Sauce* over shellfish and serve immediately.

Riesling Dill Butter Sauce

6 tbsp cold butter
4 shallots, finely chopped
2 cloves garlic, chopped

1 tsp coarsely ground black pepper
1/4 cup dry Riesling
salt

In small saucepan over medium-high heat, melt 1 tbsp butter. Sauté shallots and garlic in butter for 2 to 3 minutes or until tender and transparent. Add black pepper and Riesling. Continue to cook until liquid is reduced by half.

Using whisk, incorporate remaining cold butter into sauce. Be careful not to boil at this point or the sauce will separate. Season to taste.

Chardonnay-Vine-Skewered Shrimp and Pineapple with Chile Lime Rub

SERVES 4 TO 6

The size of the shrimp help make this first course the dramatic presentation it is – the bigger, the better. Any type of dried grapevine will do for this recipe but if grapevines are unavailable, use wooden skewers that have been soaked in Chardonnay for about an hour.

16 Chardonnay-vine skewers (about 6–8 inches long)
16 jumbo shrimp (approximately 1 lb), peeled and deveined
1 tsp sesame oil
1/4 cup rice wine vinegar
juice of 1 lime
2 tbsp honey
2 fresh chiles, seeded and chopped
1 tbsp chopped fresh ginger
1 tbsp chopped fresh coriander
Bone Dust Barbecue Spice (page 15)
1 fresh pineapple, peeled, left whole with top intact

Soak the Chardonnay-vine skewers in warm water for 1 hour. Thread 1 shrimp on end of each skewer lengthwise, from tail to head.

In small bowl, whisk together sesame oil, rice wine vinegar, lime juice and honey. Add chiles, ginger and coriander. Place shrimp skewers in shallow glass dish, pour marinade over shrimp and let marinate for 15 minutes.

Preheat grill to medium-high. Remove shrimp from marinade (reserving marinade for basting) and season to taste with *Bone Dust Barbecue Spice*. Grill shrimp for 2 to 3 minutes per side, basting frequently with reserved marinade until shrimp are opaque and tender. Stick skewers into peeled pineapple and serve.

Maple-Planked Brie with Roasted Garlic and Peppers

Make this treat for your next dinner gathering and get ready for the accolades. Although baked brie may be familiar, the method of planking is unusual, and a whole planked cheese makes quite the spectacular appetizer. The combination of melted cheese and garlicky topping smeared onto great bread is terrifically good. You can easily make the topping the day before and refrigerate it until needed; let it warm to room temperature before adding to the cheese.

SERVES 8 TO 12

1 maple plank, soaked

2 small wheels brie (1/4 lb each)

2 heads garlic, separated and peeled

1/2 cup plus 2 tbsp olive oil

2 green onions, finely chopped

1 red bell pepper, roasted, peeled, seeded and finely chopped

2 tbsp chopped fresh thyme

2 tbsp balsamic vinegar

2 tsp coarsely ground black pepper

salt

Preheat grill to high.

With sharp knife, scrape rind off the top of each wheel of brie to expose cheese. Set aside.

Heat 1/2 cup olive oil in small sauté pan and add whole cloves of garlic. Reduce heat to medium and simmer garlic in oil until softened and beginning to color, about 20 minutes. Remove from heat and, using slotted spoon, transfer garlic to small bowl to cool. Reserve garlic-flavored oil for another use. Mash garlic cloves using back of fork. Add green onions, red pepper, thyme, balsamic vinegar, 2 tbsp olive oil and black pepper. Season with salt to taste. Spread garlic and pepper mixture over tops of brie wheels.

Place soaked plank on grill, close lid and bake for 10 minutes or until it begins to crackle and smoke. Being careful of smoke, open lid and place cheeses on plank. Close lid and plank-bake for 10 to 12 minutes until cheese begins to melt and bubble. Remove planked cheese from grill. Serve with slices of crusty bread, flat bread or crudités.

Cedar-Planked Onion and Portobello Mushroom Focaccia

Think of this as a meatless muffuletta – the hero-style specialty sandwich made famous by the Central Grocery in New Orleans. In our version, we combine onions, garlic, fresh herbs and hefty portobello mushroom caps – all planked – with mellow goat cheese and fresh arugula as a filling for warm focaccia. Soaking mushrooms before planking helps tenderize them.

SERVES 4 TO 6

1 cedar plank, soaked
2 large Spanish onions, thinly sliced
2 cloves garlic, chopped
1 tbsp *Bone Dust Barbecue Spice*
    (page 15)
4 tbsp olive oil, plus extra for drizzling
salt and freshly ground pepper
4 large portobello mushroom caps

3 tbsp balsamic vinegar, plus extra
    for drizzling
2 cloves garlic, chopped
1 tbsp chopped fresh rosemary
1 tsp coarsely ground black pepper
1 round focaccia (8 inches in diameter)
1/4 lb goat cheese
1 bunch arugula, rinsed and dried

Preheat oven to 450°F. Place cedar plank in roasting pan or ovenproof dish large enough to accommodate it and add enough water to just float the plank. Place roasting pan with plank in oven and preheat for 10 minutes.

While plank is preheating, combine sliced onions, garlic, *Bone Dust* and 2 tbsp olive oil. Season with salt and pepper to taste. Place onion mixture on plank and bake for 30 minutes. After 15 minutes, turn onions (they should be starting to slightly char) and check water level in roasting pan.

While onions continue to cook, wipe mushroom caps clean with damp cloth. Fill small bowl with warm water and soak mushrooms for 5 minutes. In small bowl, combine remaining 2 tbsp olive oil, balsamic vinegar, garlic, rosemary and black pepper. Season with salt to taste. Dip each mushroom cap into balsamic vinegar mixture allowing mixture to fill gills of the caps. When onions have been in oven 30 minutes, place mushroom caps, gill-side down, on top of onions and continue to cook for 20 more minutes. Remove pan from oven, let cool slightly, then thinly slice each mushroom cap. In large bowl, toss together onions and sliced mushrooms. Season to taste and set to one side.

Turn on oven broiler. Cut focaccia horizontally into 2 rounds and drizzle the inside of each with oil and vinegar. Place bread beneath broiler for a minute or two until it is toasted golden brown. Remove from oven, spread the goat cheese evenly over one half of the bread, and top with the onion-mushroom mixture. Neatly pile arugula on top of onion-mushroom mixture and top with other half of bread. Press down slightly, cut into pieces and serve.

Plank-Smoked Garlic Risotto with Taleggio and Peas

SERVES 8

Just about any food can be improved and any flavor intensified through the use of planking. This recipe will rate as one of the best risottos you've ever tasted and it works equally well using an outdoor grill or a conventional oven.

1 cedar plank, soaked
4 heads garlic
1/4 cup butter
4 shallots, finely chopped
2 cups arborio rice
1 cup white wine
5 cups chicken broth
1/4 cup freshly grated Parmesan cheese
1/2 cup small pieces of Taleggio cheese
1 tbsp chopped fresh thyme
1 cup petits pois (frozen are fine; thaw and drain)
salt and freshly ground pepper

Preheat grill to high. Place soaked plank on grill and heat for 3 to 5 minutes or until it begins to crackle and smoke.

Cut tops off each head of garlic and peel off the excess skin. Place garlic on plank. Close lid and plank-bake for 20 to 30 minutes until garlic is soft. Remove garlic from plank and let cool. To remove smoked garlic from skin, hold heads upside down over a dish and squeeze firmly. Use metal skewer to poke out any remaining cloves. Set to one side.

Bring chicken broth to a rolling boil in a saucepan. Reduce heat to a rippling simmer, but keep hot. In large, heavy saucepan over medium heat, melt butter. Add shallots and sauté until soft and transparent. Add smoked garlic and continue to cook for 2 to 3 minutes.

Increase heat and add rice and stir until grains are well coated with butter (about 30 seconds). Add wine and continue to cook, stirring constantly, until wine is absorbed by rice.

Add hot chicken broth to rice, about 1 cup at a time, stirring after each addition until the liquid is fully absorbed. Continue until all broth is absorbed and rice is tender but still a little firm at heart, about 15 to 20 minutes. Add thyme, Parmesan, Taleggio and peas. Heat through for a few seconds, season to taste and serve immediately.

Newfoundland Cod Cakes on the Rocks with Bonavista Tartar Sauce

The inspiration for this recipe came from Ted's mom, Astrida Reader, who, after immigrating to Newfoundland from Latvia met Ted's father, Alex. "Married to my Newfie dad, Mom had to learn how to make fishcakes!" These are the best.

SERVES 8

1 piece granite
2 lb fresh cod fillets (uncooked)
3 green onions, finely chopped
1 small red onion, diced
1 red bell pepper, seeded and diced
1 tbsp *Bone Dust Barbecue Spice* (page 15)
1 tbsp chopped fresh dill
1 cup mayonnaise
1 tbsp fresh lemon juice
1-1/2 cups coarsely crushed soda crackers
salt and freshly ground pepper
Bonavista Tartar Sauce (recipe follows)

Preheat oven to 425°F. Place granite in oven on middle rack and preheat for 20 minutes.

Place cod in large mixing bowl and shred into small pieces with your fingers. Add remaining ingredients and blend together with fork. Shape mixture into 8 round cakes.

Transfer cod cakes to preheated granite and bake for 12 to 15 minutes until heated through and cooked. Serve with *Bonavista Tartar Sauce* and mixed baby greens.

Bonavista (a.k.a. Ted's Mom's) Tartar Sauce

2 cups homemade or quality store-bought mayonnaise

1/2 cup homemade or store-bought zucchini relish

1 tsp coarsely ground black pepper

1 tbsp lemon juice

2 tsp chopped fresh dill

salt

In mixing bowl, whisk together mayonnaise, zucchini relish, pepper, lemon juice and dill. Season with salt to taste. Cover and refrigerate for 1 to 2 hours to allow flavors to develop.

Black-Peppered Quail on Cinnamon Sticks with Wheat Berry and Smoked-Bacon Salad

The most natural of skewers, cinnamon sticks are just the thing to use to spear delicate quail flesh. Choose the thinnest sticks you can find and, if you wish, soak them for an hour ahead of time in a little Frangelico (hazelnut liqueur) or cinnamon-flavored liqueur.

SERVES 6

12 cinnamon sticks, soaked
2 tsp ground cinnamon
2 tbsp coarsely ground black pepper
2 tbsp chopped fresh ginger
1 tsp five-spice powder
1/4 cup rice wine vinegar
1/4 cup vegetable oil
12 quail, boned
Wheat Berry and Smoked-Bacon Salad (recipe follows)

In bowl, whisk together cinnamon, black pepper, ginger, five-spice powder, rice wine vinegar and oil. Season with salt to taste. Set to one side.

Lay 2 quail side by side, not touching, on a work surface. Skewer through both quail at leg ends with one cinnamon stick, and through wing ends with a second cinnamon stick. (The 2 sticks help to keep quail flat.) Repeat this process until you have 6 double quail kebabs with 2 quail on each pair of sticks.

Pour half of the marinade into shallow glass dish, place skewers in marinade, and pour remaining marinade over quail. Cover with plastic wrap and refrigerate for 4 hours.

Preheat grill to medium-high. Grill quail skewers for 3 to 4 minutes per side to medium doneness, basting with marinade. (Note: quail do not need to be cooked to well done.) Remove from heat, carefully extract cinnamon sticks and serve quail with *Wheat Berry and Smoked-Bacon Salad* (recipe follows) and *Cedar-Roasted Shallot and Shiitake Polenta* (page 19).

Wheat Berry and Smoked-Bacon Salad

Quinoa or barley may be used in place of wheat berries.

1-1/2 cups wheat berries, soaked in water overnight
1/2 lb double-smoked bacon, diced
2 ears fresh corn
1 mild-tasting onion (such as Vidalia), diced
1/2 cup peas (if frozen, thaw and drain)
1 red bell pepper, seeded and diced
1 tbsp chopped fresh oregano
2 cloves garlic, chopped
1 tsp *Bone Dust Barbecue Spice* (page 15)
2 tbsp red wine vinegar
1/4 cup vegetable oil
salt and freshly ground pepper

Cook wheat berries in large pot of boiling salted water, uncovered, until tender, about 1-1/2 hours. Rinse in cold water and drain well. Fry bacon in skillet until crisp. Transfer to paper towels to drain.

Preheat grill to high. Grill corn for 5 to 6 minutes until slightly charred and tender. Cool slightly, then remove kernels from cob, using sharp knife.

In bowl, combine wheat berries, bacon, corn, onions, peas, red pepper, oregano, garlic, *Bone Dust*, red wine vinegar and oil. Season with salt and pepper to taste. Chill and serve.

CHAPTER 2

From the Land

CHICKEN, BEEF, PORK,

LAMB, TURKEY, GAME

Mesquite-Planked Chicken
with Smoky Corn Salsa

Oak-Planked Honey Garlic Chicken Thighs
with Cinnamon

Cedar-Planked Turkey
with Wild Rice and Bread Stuffing

Maple-Planked Prime Rib Roast
with Honey Brown Beer and Mustard

Bacon-Wrapped Planked Beef Tenderloin
with Blue-Cheese Cobbler

Cedar-Plank Roast Rack of Pork
with Maple Tarragon Mustard Glaze

Burgundy-Vine-Skewered Beef
with Sweet Onions and Field Mushrooms

Pork Tenderloin on Applewood
with Cornbread and Sweet Potato Stuffing

Planked Crown Rack of Lamb
with Savory Stuffing

Planked Boneless Half-Chicken
with Herbs and Old Cheddar

Roll-in-the-Hay-Wrapped Steak
with Herb and Pepper Butter

Plank-Roasted Venison Strip Loin
with Balsamic Raspberry Glaze

Granite-Roasted Lamb Burgers
with Goat Cheese Onion Slaw

While the plank-cooking technique started with fresh fish and seafood on hot wood, it certainly doesn't end there. Plank-cooking lends itself extremely well to meat, poultry and game as you will discover when you begin to experiment with these dishes.

The recipes in this section run the gamut from stylish mains like *Maple-Planked Prime Rib Roast with Honey Brown Beer and Mustard* and the truly outstanding entrée of *Cedar-Plank Roast Rack of Pork with Maple Tarragon Mustard Glaze* to a stone-roasted burger in the form of *Granite-Roasted Lamb Burgers with Goat Cheese Onion Slaw*.

The benefits of planking meat are twofold. First, there is the inevitable flavor boost — which is considerable. Secondly, with this relatively quick cooking method, valuable natural juices are sealed in because the meat really doesn't have a chance to lose moisture. The inventive recipes in this chapter are enhanced with multi-layered influences of supporting ingredients such as fresh herbs and condiments, citrus and spice. Often inspired by traditional pairings, our combinations may sound exotic, but they are well grounded and not at all difficult to prepare. For example, the *Bacon-Wrapped Planked Beef Tenderloin with Blue-Cheese Cobbler* and *Pork Tenderloin on Applewood with Cornbread and Sweet Potato Stuffing*: familiar combinations — beef and bacon with a blue-cheese note, that in the past might have come in the form of an accompanying salad or baked potato topping. The pork tenderloin with cornbread stuffing is reminiscent of Sunday roast pork dinner. What could be more traditional? Yet coupled with the smoky wood, the flavors are completely different — everything old is new again!

Mesquite-Planked Chicken with Smoky Corn Salsa

The flavors of the American Southwest are the top notes in this easy recipe. We've used fresh jalapeños but you can vary the chiles according to what is available. Choose the largest chicken breasts you can find so as to have the surface necessary to accommodate the stuffing between the skin and the flesh.

2 mesquite or hickory planks, soaked
2 ears corn, shucked
1 small red onion, sliced
1 red bell pepper
2 jalapeño peppers
1 tbsp chopped fresh coriander
juice of 1 lime
2 cloves garlic, chopped
1 cup grated Monterey Jack cheese
salt and freshly ground pepper
8 large chicken breasts (6–8 oz each)
1–2 tbsp *Bone Dust Barbecue Spice* (page 15)

Preheat grill to high. Grill corn, red onion and red pepper until charred and tender, about 12 to 15 minutes. Remove from grill and let cool slightly. Using sharp knife, remove kernels of corn from each cob. Dice onions. Peel, seed and dice red pepper. Finely chop jalapeños. (Use rubber gloves when handling hot chile peppers and avoid contact with your face.) In large bowl, combine corn, onion, red pepper, jalapeño, coriander, lime juice, garlic and Monterey Jack cheese. Season to taste.

Carefully lift skin from flesh of chicken breasts, keeping skin intact and attached at edges, to form a pocket. Using small spoon, fill each pocket with corn mixture, packing in as much filling as you can. Season well with *Bone Dust*.

Place soaked planks on grill, close lid and bake for 3 to 5 minutes or until they begin to crackle and smoke. Place chicken breasts on hot planks and close lid. Plank-bake for 15 to 20 minutes until skin is golden brown and crisp and chicken is fully cooked.

Oak-Planked Honey Garlic Chicken Thighs with Cinnamon

*The humble chicken thigh is rendered supreme when combined with the magnificence of oak.
However, with its Asian overtones, we think this recipe would also work well planked on cedar.*

SERVES 8

2 oak or cedar planks, soaked
4 cloves plus 2 cloves garlic, chopped
1 tsp coarse salt
1 tbsp coarse black pepper
1 tsp plus 1/2 tsp ground cinnamon
16 skinless chicken thighs
3 tbsp butter
1 tbsp chopped fresh ginger
1 tbsp chopped fresh herbs
    (parsley, sage, rosemary, thyme)

1/2 cup honey
1 cup fresh orange juice
1/4 cup hoisin sauce
1 tbsp sesame seeds
1 tbsp cornstarch
2 tbsp cold water
salt and freshly ground pepper

In small bowl, combine 4 cloves chopped garlic, salt, pepper and 1 tsp cinnamon; mix well. Rub this mixture over chicken thighs. Place in dish, cover, and refrigerate for 2 hours.

Meanwhile make basting sauce: In medium saucepan, melt butter over medium-high heat. Add ginger, 2 cloves chopped garlic and 1/2 tsp cinnamon, and sauté for 2 to 3 minutes. Add herbs, honey, orange juice, hoisin sauce and sesame seeds. Bring to a boil, reduce heat and simmer for 3 minutes. Mix together cornstarch and cold water in cup, whisk into sauce and return to a boil and cook until thick and glossy. Reduce heat and season to taste. Let cool slightly.

Preheat grill to high. Place soaked planks on grill, close lid and bake for 3 to 5 minutes or until they begin to crackle and smoke. Carefully open lid of grill and, using tongs, place chicken thighs on planks, 8 per plank. Close lid and plank-bake for 5 minutes. Carefully open the lid and after smoke has cleared, baste thighs liberally with sauce. Close lid and continue to cook for another 5 minutes. Repeat basting, close lid and cook for another 5 minutes. After 15 to 20 minutes of planking and basting, remove plank from grill. Transfer thighs to large bowl, toss with remaining basting sauce and serve immediately.

Cedar-Planked Turkey with Wild Rice and Bread Stuffing

Once you serve a planked turkey, Thanksgiving will never be the same. This oven-plank method produces an ultra-moist, tender, deeply flavorful turkey. Monitor the level of apple cider in the roasting pan carefully to ensure it doesn't dry out.

SERVES 8 TO 10

1 cedar plank, large enough to fit
   loosely in a roasting pan
8 cups apple cider
12–16 lb fresh turkey
6 tbsp butter
4 large cloves garlic, chopped
3 Spanish onions, diced
2 or 3 stalks celery, diced

1 cup fully cooked wild rice
2 tbsp chopped fresh sage
2 tbsp chopped fresh thyme
1/2 cup sultanas or golden raisins
2 loaves thick-sliced, day-old
   white bakery bread,
   crusts removed and diced
salt and freshly ground pepper

Preheat oven to 450°F.

Place plank in roasting pan. Pour in enough apple cider to just float plank. Set aside.

Remove giblets and neck from turkey, and season cavity with a little salt and pepper. Set bird to one side while you make the dressing.

In large stock pot, melt butter over medium-high heat. Sauté garlic, onion and celery for 3 to 5 minutes until tender. Add cooked wild rice, sage, thyme and sultanas and continue to cook for 2 to 3 minutes. Add diced bread and season with salt and pepper to taste. Stir to combine everything thoroughly. Remove from heat and let cool 15 minutes. Stuff turkey cavity and neck with dressing. Skewer or sew openings closed. (If you have a little too much dressing, wrap the excess in foil and cook it alongside the turkey for the last half-hour of roasting.)

Place roasting pan with plank in oven and preheat for 15 minutes. Rub turkey with a little salt and pepper, place on wire rack and set in roasting pan on top of the plank. Plank-roast for 30 minutes to sear, then reduce heat to 325°F. Loosely cover turkey with foil and continue to plank-roast for 3-1/2 to 4 hours (approximately 20 minutes per pound). Baste frequently (using a bulb baster to make it easier) with pan juices and carefully monitor level of apple cider in roasting pan. During last hour of cooking remove foil to crisp and brown skin.

Maple-Planked Prime Rib Roast with Honey Brown Beer and Mustard

Beer and beef make great partners, especially when combined in this fashion.

1 maple plank, large enough to fit loosely in a roasting pan
5 bottles (12 fl oz each) honey brown lager beer
6 lb prime rib roast
4 cloves garlic, chopped
2 tbsp *Bone Dust Barbecue Spice* (page 15)
2 tbsp coarsely ground black pepper
2 tsp coarse salt
1/2 cup wholegrain Dijon mustard
1/2 cup pure maple syrup
2 tbsp chopped fresh thyme
salt

Preheat oven to 450°F.

Place plank in roasting pan and pour 2 bottles of beer over plank until it just floats. Set aside.

In small bowl, combine garlic, *Bone Dust*, black pepper and salt. Rub this mixture into prime rib pressing firmly into flesh. Set to one side.

In large saucepan, bring another 2 bottles of beer to a rolling boil. Reduce heat to low and simmer for 15 minutes until liquid is reduced by half. Add mustard, maple syrup and thyme. Season with salt to taste.

Place roasting pan with plank in oven for 10 minutes to preheat. Place seasoned beef directly on plank. Plank-roast for 15 minutes, then reduce heat to 350°F and continue to roast for 1-1/2 to 1-3/4 hours for medium-rare doneness (approximately 20 minutes per pound). While beef is plank-roasting, baste liberally and frequently with beer and mustard mixture and use remaining beer to top up level of liquid in roasting pan as needed. When beef is done, remove from oven, cover loosely with foil and let rest for 15 minutes before carving.

Bacon-Wrapped Planked Beef Tenderloin with Blue-Cheese Cobbler

Our blue-cheese cobbler is an imaginative spin on the traditional sweet dessert cobbler. Croutons and blue cheese are combined with onions and a blend of fresh herbs to make a fitting crown for elegant beef tenderloin. Reserve this dish for a special occasion.

1 hickory plank, soaked
6 slices bacon
6 beef tenderloin steaks (6 oz each)
2 tbsp *Bone Dust Barbecue Spice* (page 15)
1/4 cup bourbon
2 tbsp olive oil
2 tbsp plus 1/4 cup chopped fresh herbs
   (parsley, sage, rosemary, thyme)
1 tbsp cracked black pepper
1/4 lb blue cheese, softened
1 small onion, diced
2 tbsp balsamic vinegar
1 cup croutons
salt and freshly ground pepper

In skillet, sauté bacon for 3 to 4 minutes until half cooked. Transfer to paper towels and pat dry to remove excess fat. Let cool.

In small bowl, whisk together *Bone Dust*, bourbon, olive oil, 2 tbsp fresh herbs and cracked black pepper. Season steaks with this mixture then wrap a piece of bacon around each steak, securing with toothpick. Cover steaks with plastic wrap and marinate in refrigerator for 2 hours.

Meanwhile, make cobbler: In bowl, combine softened blue cheese with onion, 1/4 cup herbs and vinegar. Slightly crush croutons (use rolling pin and waxed paper) and fold into blue-cheese mixture. Season to taste. Form into 6 patties each about the same size as the steaks. Set to one side.

Preheat grill to high. Place soaked planks on grill, close lid and bake for 3 to 5 minutes or until they begin to crackle and smoke. Carefully open lid and place steaks on planks. Plank-bake for 7 to 9 minutes, carefully open lid, turn steaks and continue baking for another 7 to 9 minutes for medium doneness. During the final 3 to 5 minutes of planking, place 1 blue-cheese patty on top of each steak and cook long enough to allow cheese to develop crust. Serve immediately.

Cedar-Plank Roast Rack of Pork with Maple Tarragon Mustard Glaze

Because today's pork is bred to be ultra-lean, it has a tendency to dry out if overcooked. This method of plank-roasting over apple cider ensures a beautifully moist and quite delicious pork roast. For optimum results, follow the cooking times to the letter.

SERVES 6

1 maple plank, large enough to fit loosely in a roasting pan
4 cups apple cider
2 cinnamon sticks, broken into pieces
6 cloves
6 cardamom pods
6- to 8-rib rack of pork loin
2 tbsp cracked black pepper
2 tsp coarse salt
2 cloves garlic, chopped
2 tbsp chopped fresh tarragon
1/4 cup maple syrup
2 tbsp wholegrain Dijon mustard

Preheat oven to 500°F.

Place plank in roasting pan. Pour apple cider over plank just until it floats. Add cinnamon, cloves and cardamom to cider. Set aside.

Using sharp knife, diamond score top of pork loin about 1/2-inch deep. Season with pepper and salt, rubbing well into meat. In small bowl, combine garlic, tarragon, maple syrup and mustard and mix well. Set to one side.

Place roasting pan with plank in oven to preheat for 10 minutes.

Place rack of pork on plank. Sear for 15 minutes, then reduce heat to 375°F and continue plank-roasting for 1 hour. Check level of cider occasionally and add more as needed. After 1 hour, start to baste pork with maple-mustard mixture. Continue to plank-roast for another 10 to 15 minutes. Remove pork from oven, baste once again, then let it rest for 10 to 15 minutes before carving. (Meat should have a touch of pink to it.) Slice into large rack chops and serve with remaining basting sauce.

Burgundy-Vine-Skewered Beef with Sweet Onions and Field Mushrooms

All beef on one skewer and all vegetables on the other – that's the foolproof way to ensure even cooking times for both. If you can't locate Burgundy vines, soak wooden skewers in Burgundy for an hour or so before using.

SERVES 8

16 Burgundy vines (about 12 inches
    long) soaked in water for an hour
1 cup Burgundy red wine
1/4 cup plus 2 tbsp olive oil
4 cloves garlic, chopped
1 medium onion, diced
2 tbsp chopped fresh rosemary
2 tbsp green peppercorns in brine,
    drained and crushed
2 tbsp Dijon mustard

1 tbsp juniper berries
4 lb beef sirloin, cut into 2-inch cubes
2 medium zucchini
2 red bell peppers, halved, seeded
2 yellow bell peppers, halved, seeded
2 medium red onions, peeled
24 cremini or shiitake mushrooms,
    wiped clean
1/4 cup balsamic vinegar
salt and freshly ground pepper

In large bowl, combine wine, 1/4 cup olive oil, garlic, onion, rosemary, green peppercorns, mustard and juniper berries. Mix well. Add beef cubes, toss to coat well, cover with plastic wrap and refrigerate for 4 to 6 hours. After marinating, thread beef onto 8 vine skewers. Set to one side. Reserve the marinade.

Preheat grill to high.

Cut zucchini, red and yellow peppers and red onions into large pieces. Skewer onto remaining 8 vine skewers alternating with mushrooms. In small bowl, combine 2 tbsp olive oil and balsamic vinegar. Brush vegetables with this mixture and season to taste.

Grill beef skewers for 2 to 3 minutes per side (8 to 10 minutes total cooking time for medium-rare doneness) basting frequently with remaining marinade. When beef has been cooking 3 minutes, place vegetable skewers on grill and cook for 6 to 8 minutes until tender, brushing with remaining oil and vinegar mixture. Remove from grill and serve.

Pork Tenderloin on Applewood with Cornbread and Sweet Potato Stuffing

Designed for cold-weather appetites, this substantial recipe combines the richness of pork tenderloin with a savory stuffing. Make the cornbread a couple of days in advance (store-bought corn muffins are fine, too) so that it will be somewhat dry.

SERVES 4 TO 6

1 applewood plank, soaked
butcher's twine
1–1-1/2 lb fresh pork tenderloin
salt and freshly ground pepper
1 tbsp wholegrain Dijon mustard
Cornbread and Sweet Potato Stuffing (recipe follows)
Cider Glaze (recipe follows)

Using sharp knife, slice pork tenderloin lengthwise about 3/4 through. Splay tenderloin out, butterfly fashion. Cover with plastic wrap and, using kitchen mallet, gently pound the tenderloin flat to form a sort of large rectangle. Season with salt and pepper to taste and spread evenly with mustard. Set to one side while you prepare stuffing and cider glaze.

Preheat oven to 400°F. Place plank in roasting pan and pour in apple cider until it just floats. Preheat in oven for 15 minutes.

Arrange cooled stuffing along length of tenderloin, pressing it firmly into place in shape of log. Carefully roll up pork to form tight cylinder. Using butcher's twine, tie pork in 6 or 7 sections to keep it together. Season with salt and pepper to taste. Place stuffed pork tenderloin on plank and roast for 40 to 45 minutes basting every 10 minutes with cider glaze. Remove pan from oven and let meat rest for 10 minutes before slicing into 1-inch rounds. Serve with remaining glaze.

Cornbread and Sweet Potato Stuffing

1 large sweet potato, peeled and diced
3 tbsp vegetable oil
1 medium onion, diced
1 leek, rinsed, trimmed and diced
1 red pepper, seeded and diced
2 jalapeño peppers, seeded and diced
   (use rubber gloves)

2 tbsp chopped fresh coriander
3 tbsp rice wine vinegar
2 cups dry cornbread cubes
salt and freshly ground pepper

In saucepan, cook diced sweet potato in 3 cups boiling water for 5 to 7 minutes until tender. Drain and cool. In skillet, heat oil over medium-high heat and sauté onion and leek for 4 to 5 minutes until tender. Add cooked sweet potato, red pepper, jalapeño and coriander and continue to cook for another 5 minutes. Add rice wine vinegar and cook until liquid is mostly evaporated. Remove from heat and transfer to large bowl. Add cornbread cubes to bowl and mix thoroughly with your hands, firmly pressing mixture together. Season with salt and pepper to taste. Let cool.

Cider Glaze

3 cups apple cider
2 tbsp wholegrain Dijon mustard
1/4 cup chilled butter, cut in pieces
salt and freshly ground pepper

In saucepan, bring cider to a rolling boil, reduce heat to medium and let simmer for 30 minutes until cider has reduced in volume to 1 cup. Using whisk, blend in mustard and chilled butter. Whisk until butter is fully incorporated. Remove from heat, season with salt and pepper to taste. Let cool.

Planked Crown Rack of Lamb with Savory Stuffing

If you are a dab hand at this sort of thing, buy two large racks of lamb – either Australian or American (which are the largest) – and tie them together to make a crown rack. Otherwise, ask your butcher to do it for you. This presentation will knock your guests' collective socks off!

1 cedar plank, soaked
2 tbsp cracked black pepper
4 cloves garlic, chopped, divided
2 tbsp chopped fresh rosemary, divided
1 tsp coarse salt
2 tbsp olive oil
1 crown roast rack of lamb
1 medium onion, diced
1 lb ground lamb
2 tbsp Dijon mustard
2 tbsp Worcestershire sauce
1 tbsp summer savory
3 cups dry white bread cubes
salt and freshly ground pepper

In small bowl, combine pepper, garlic, rosemary, salt and olive oil. Rub all over and well into lamb. Set to one side.

In mixing bowl, combine onion, garlic, ground lamb, Dijon mustard, Worcestershire sauce, rosemary and bread cubes. Using your hands, mix ingredients together well. Firmly pack stuffing into cavity of crown roast of lamb.

Preheat oven to 425°F. Place plank on baking sheet and preheat in oven for 10 minutes. Place lamb on plank and plank-roast for 40 to 45 minutes for medium-rare doneness. Remove from oven and let rest for 10 minutes before carving and serving.

Planked Boneless Half-Chicken with Herbs and Old Cheddar

Because the half-chickens are boned and splayed out, they cook quite quickly on the plank and come away infused with great flavor. All you need is a vibrantly dressed salad of baby greens, boiled new potatoes tossed with butter and chives and maybe a simple (unoaked!) Chablis to complete the meal. Ask the butcher to bone the chickens for you.

SERVES 4 TO 8

2 cedar planks, soaked
4 boneless half-chickens, skin on and breast and legs attached
salt and freshly ground pepper
1-1/2 cups grated old white Cheddar cheese
3 shallots, finely chopped
1/4 cup chopped fresh herbs (parsley, sage, rosemary, thyme)
2 tsp coarsely ground black pepper
2 tbsp white wine vinegar, plus extra for brushing
juice of 1/2 lemon and 1 orange (for brushing)
rosemary branch

Lay chickens on a flat, clean work surface and season with salt and pepper on both sides. Turn them skin-side down and, working from center of chicken, carefully lift meat away from skin to form pocket. Make sure you leave skin intact and attached to meat at edges.

In bowl, combine cheese, shallots, herbs, pepper and vinegar. Season with salt to taste. Divide mixture into 4 equal parts and stuff 1 portion between meat and skin of each half-chicken, pressing firmly. Transfer to plate, cover with plastic wrap and refrigerate for 1 hour to allow meat and stuffing to firm up a little.

Preheat grill to high. Place soaked planks on grill, close lid and bake for 3 to 5 minutes until they begin to crackle and smoke. Carefully open lid and place 2 stuffed half-chickens on each plank, meat-side down. Close lid and plank-bake for 18 to 20 minutes until chicken is cooked and the skin is golden and crisp. From time to time check the plank (extinguish any flames with a spray bottle) and brush chicken with rosemary branch brush dipped in a mixture of lemon juice, orange juice and white wine vinegar. Serve immediately.

Roll-in-the-Hay-Wrapped Steak with Herb and Pepper Butter

Straight from the chef's mouth: "This is a little bizarre, but lots of fun! It's a bit tricky so I would recommend it only to someone who really knows their way around a grill. You must be extremely careful. The hay definitely does catch fire so it must be done in a very open, safe area – not on a balcony!" Make the Herb and Pepper Butter *ahead of time.*

SERVES 6

1/4 bale green hay, soaked for 1/2 hour
    in 3–4 bottles (12 fl oz each) beer
2 cloves garlic, chopped
2 tbsp *Bone Dust Barbecue Spice*
    (page 15)
1/4 cup chopped fresh herbs
    (parsley, sage, rosemary, thyme)

1/4 cup molasses
2 tbsp balsamic vinegar
2 tbsp coarsely ground black pepper
salt
6 strip loin steaks (8 oz each)
Herb and Pepper Butter (recipe follows)

Preheat grill to high.

In bowl, combine garlic, *Bone Dust*, herbs, molasses, vinegar, black pepper and salt to taste. Rub mixture well into steaks, pressing firmly into meat. Shake off excess liquid from a good handful of hay; lay flat on a work surface and spread out evenly to approximate length of each steak. Place one steak at bottom end and carefully roll up. Repeat for remaining steaks. (You should have about half of the hay left in the bucket.)

Place hay-wrapped steaks right on grill and close lid. Expect a lot of smoke after about 2 minutes! Carefully lift lid, turn steaks over and cover loosely with remaining soaked hay. Continue to cook for another 2 to 3 minutes for medium-rare doneness. Open lid to burn off hay and sear steaks. (Note: the more often you lift the lid, the faster the hay will burn as it is being fed oxygen. The burning of the hay sears the steaks, so don't lift the lid repeatedly.) Serve with *Herb and Pepper Butter*.

Herb and Pepper Butter

1/2 lb butter, softened
1/4 cup chopped fresh herbs
    (parsley, sage, rosemary, thyme)

2 tbsp coarsely ground black pepper
2 tbsp balsamic vinegar
4 shallots, finely chopped

MAKES APPROXIMATELY 1-1/2 CUPS

In bowl, blend butter, herbs, black pepper, balsamic vinegar and shallots. Season with salt to taste. Transfer to small container and refrigerate until needed. (Note: this butter can be kept in the freezer for up to 8 weeks.)

Plank-Roasted Venison Strip Loin with Balsamic Raspberry Glaze

SERVES 8

This is a big, bold-flavored planking dish, so you can team it with similarly bold sides – try the Stuffed Twice-Baked Smoked Potatoes *(page 76) and the* Plank-Roasted Root Vegetables *(page 83). Make the* Balsamic Raspberry Glaze *at the start. The length of the strip loin will determine the length of the plank. Use any hardwood.*

1 or 2 oak planks, soaked

2–3 lb venison strip loin,
    silver skin scraped away

2 tbsp cracked black pepper

1/4 cup wholegrain Dijon mustard

2 tbsp each thyme, parsley, chopped

2 tbsp balsamic vinegar

2 tbsp olive oil

coarse salt for plank

Balsamic Raspberry Glaze (recipe follows)

Rub venison well with cracked black pepper. In bowl, combine mustard, thyme, parsley, balsamic vinegar and olive oil. Place venison in glass dish and pour mustard marinade over meat, making sure meat is well covered on all sides. Cover with plastic wrap and marinate in refrigerator for 3 to 4 hours. Allow meat to come to room temperature before planking.

Preheat grill to high. Place soaked plank on grill, close lid and bake for 3 to 5 minutes until it begins to crackle and smoke. Carefully open lid and season plank with coarse salt. Remove venison from marinade and, using your hands, wipe away excess marinade. Place venison on plank and baste with *Balsamic Raspberry Glaze*. Close lid and plank-roast for 15 to 18 minutes (for medium doneness), basting 2 or 3 times with glaze. Allow venison to rest for 5 minutes before slicing. Serve with remaining glaze.

Balsamic Raspberry Glaze

2 tbsp olive oil

2 cloves garlic, chopped

3 shallots, diced

1/2 cup balsamic vinegar

3 cups fresh raspberries

1 cup light-bodied beef broth

2 sprigs fresh thyme

1 tsp cracked black pepper and salt

In medium saucepan, sauté garlic and shallots for 2 to 3 minutes in olive oil until tender and transparent. Pour balsamic vinegar into pan to deglaze it, scraping up brown bits. Boil gently and continue stirring until liquid is reduced by half. Add raspberries and continue to cook for another 3 minutes, stirring and slightly mashing raspberries to extract juice. Add beef broth, thyme and black pepper. Bring to boil and reduce heat to medium. Let simmer for 15 to 20 minutes to reduce liquid by half. In blender or food processor, purée until smooth. Strain, season with salt and let cool.

Granite-Roasted Lamb Burgers with Goat Cheese Onion Slaw

The evolution – and elevation – of the burger!

1 piece granite
1-1/2 lb ground lamb
1/2 lb ground pork
3 cloves garlic, finely chopped
1 medium onion, finely chopped
1 tbsp chopped fresh rosemary

2 tbsp Dijon mustard
1 tbsp *Bone Dust Barbecue Spice*
    (page 15)
1 tsp coarse salt
Goat Cheese Onion Slaw (recipe follows)

Preheat oven to 425°F. Place granite in oven to preheat for 15 minutes.

In mixing bowl, combine lamb, pork, garlic, onion, rosemary, Dijon mustard, *Bone Dust* and salt. Shape burger mixture into 8 patties. Place patties on granite and oven-roast for 15 minutes, until crisp outside and medium to medium-well inside. Remove from oven and serve with split, fresh baguettes and *Goat Cheese Onion Slaw*.

Goat Cheese Onion Slaw

1 medium red onion, thinly sliced
1 medium yellow onion, thinly sliced
4 green onions, diced
2 tbsp extra virgin olive oil

2 tbsp red wine vinegar
4–6 oz goat cheese, softened
1 tbsp chopped fresh mint
salt and freshly ground pepper

MAKES
APPROXIMATELY
2 CUPS

In mixing bowl, combine onions, olive oil, vinegar and mint and mix thoroughly. Using large fork, blend goat cheese into onion mixture until well incorporated. Season to taste. Serve with *Granite-Roasted Lamb Burgers* as a side dish.

CHAPTER 3

From the Sea

FISH AND SEAFOOD

Oak-Planked Pistachio-Crusted Sea Scallops

Cedar-Planked Salmon Fillets
with Shallot and Dill Crust

Grouper Wrapped in Banana Leaves
with Chipotle Chile Lime Butter

Chinook Salmon on Alderwood
with Vidalia Onion and Mustard Crust

Cedar-Planked Arctic Char with
Summer Savory and Partridge Berry Relish

Planked Halibut Fillets with
Green Onion Paste and Roasted Lemon Butter

Granite-Roasted Pickerel
with Lemon Pepper Ricotta Crust

Cedar-Planked Atlantic Lobster Cakes
with Curry Citrus Mayo

Pancetta-Wrapped Oysters on Chardonnay Vines
with Roasted Garlic Sauce

Pine-Needle-Smoked Mussels

Planked Sea Bass
with Cuban Mojito Sauce

In 1857 American author Eliza Leslie included a recipe for *Planked Great Lakes Whitefish* in her *New Cookery Book*, and she described the cooking method for fish as "superior to all others." In 1896 the renowned Fanny Farmer discussed the merits of planking, pointing out that her own planks "had been used long and often, gaining virtue with every planking." (Those must have been some serious planks!)

Eliza and Fanny clearly knew a good thing when it came along. When you first taste planked fish you may have precisely the same reaction. Far from being a culinary hit-or-miss proposition (often the case with fresh fish and seafood cooked directly on the grill), planked fish retain the natural juices and oils and emerge self-basted and infused with the flavors of the smoke. Once the fish or seafood are placed on the planks, there is no need to move or turn the fish. The hot wood and the grill do the rest. Your only concern will be to keep an eye on the grill and extinguish any flames as they occur. The inherent layers of complex flavors and textures in sumptuous fish such as salmon and sweet shellfish such as shrimp, lobster or scallops simply spring to life with this method of roasting.

Oak-Planked Pistachio-Crusted Sea Scallops

We have often enjoyed the scallops coated in ground pistachios at Toronto's Splendido Bar and Grill. Chef and owner Arpi Magyar has had a pan-roasted version of them on the menu from day one. Thus inspired, may we present the only scallop dish we've tasted to better them? Make sure to use undyed pistachios for this dish or your scallops will emerge bright pink!

SERVES 4

1 oak plank, soaked
1 cup ground pistachio nuts
3 cloves garlic, chopped
2 green onions, finely chopped
2 tbsp chopped fresh sorrel
2 tsp dry mustard
2 tbsp honey
2 tbsp fresh lemon juice
2 tbsp olive oil
sea salt and freshly ground pepper
12 large sea scallops (of uniform size)

Preheat grill to high.

In mixing bowl, combine ground pistachio nuts, garlic, green onion, sorrel, mustard, honey, lemon juice and olive oil. Whisk together to blend well. Season to taste.

Using paper towel, pat dry each of the scallops then season with sea salt and pepper.

Dip top of each scallop into pistachio mixture to crust it well. Set to one side.

Place soaked plank on grill, close lid and bake for 3 to 5 minutes until it begins to crackle and smoke. Carefully open the lid and place scallops crust side up on plank about 1/2 inch apart. Close lid and plank-bake for 6 to 8 minutes until flesh of scallops is golden brown and crust is crispy. Remove from grill and serve immediately with *Cedar-Roasted Garlic Aïoli* (page 80).

Cedar-Planked Salmon Fillets with Shallot and Dill Crust

This is the recipe that kick-started this book. If you have a strong love of salmon, you owe it to yourself to make it at least once. After that, you'll likely prefer it over any other salmon recipe. We don't think it's possible to give quality salmon a finer treatment than this.

SERVES 8

2 cedar planks, soaked
8 skinless fillets of Atlantic salmon,
    about 2 inches thick (6 oz each)
sea salt
1 cup chopped fresh dill
1/2 cup chopped shallots
2 cloves garlic, chopped
2 green onions, chopped
3 tbsp cracked black pepper
juice of 1 lemon
1 tbsp *Bone Dust Barbecue Spice* (page 15)
2 tbsp olive oil
1 large lemon for squeezing

Preheat grill to high.

Season salmon fillets with sea salt and set to one side. In bowl, combine dill, shallots, garlic, green onion, black pepper, lemon juice, *Bone Dust* and olive oil. Blend together well. Use this mixture to form crust on flesh side (not skin side) of each salmon fillet.

Season soaked planks with sea salt and place on grill, close lid and heat for 3 to 5 minutes until they start to

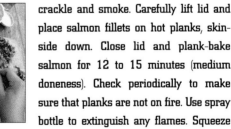

crackle and smoke. Carefully lift lid and place salmon fillets on hot planks, skin-side down. Close lid and plank-bake salmon for 12 to 15 minutes (medium doneness). Check periodically to make sure that planks are not on fire. Use spray bottle to extinguish any flames. Squeeze lemon over all fillets. Carefully remove planks from grill, and using metal spatula, transfer salmon fillets to serving platter. Serve immediately.

Grouper Wrapped in Banana Leaves with Chipotle Chile Lime Butter

This recipe is inspired by another traditional method of cooking fish. In Mexico it is very common to wrap fresh red snapper in banana leaves and cook it on a makeshift wooden frame over a beach fire. Look for banana leaves at Latin American or South American markets. Make the Chipotle Chile Lime Butter *ahead of time as you will need it for this recipe.*

2 large banana leaves, cut into
    12-inch squares (6 squares needed)
3 tbsp *Bone Dust Barbecue Spice* (page 15)
6 fresh grouper fillets (6 oz each)
1 ripe mango, peeled and thinly sliced
1 red bell pepper, thinly sliced
1 yellow bell pepper, thinly sliced
1 red onion, thinly sliced
juice of 1 lime
2 tbsp chopped fresh coriander
sea salt and freshly ground pepper
3/4 cup *Chipotle Chile Lime Butter* (recipe follows)

Preheat grill to medium-high.

Season grouper fillets with *Bone Dust* and set to one side. In mixing bowl, combine mango, red and yellow pepper, red onion, lime juice and coriander, mixing together thoroughly. Season with salt and pepper to taste. Set to one side.

Lay one square of banana leaf on flat work surface. Spoon a portion of the mango mixture onto middle of leaf, place one seasoned grouper fillet on mango mixture, top with 2 tbsp *Chipotle Chile Lime Butter* and finish with another portion of mango. Tightly wrap up the grouper in the leaf: start at bottom, then bring in sides, fold over top, and press firmly to seal the package. You may tie the bundles with butcher's twine. Repeat this process with the remaining fillets of grouper. Place fish bundles on grill and cook for 6 to 8 minutes per side, turning once. Using tongs, carefully remove from grill. Let sit for a few moments and unwrap. Serve with extra *Chipotle Chile Lime Butter* if you wish.

Chipotle Chile Lime Butter

1/2 lb butter, softened
1/4 cup canned chipotle chiles, puréed
juice of 1 lime
1 tbsp chopped fresh coriander
1/2 tsp ground cumin seed
sea salt and freshly ground pepper

MAKES
APPROXIMATELY
1-1/2 CUPS

In bowl, combine butter, chipotle purée, lime juice, coriander and cumin. Blend all ingredients together well. Season with salt to taste. Transfer to small container and refrigerate until needed.

Chinook Salmon on Alderwood with Vidalia Onion and Mustard Crust

SERVES 8

Pacific salmon (among the best is Chinook) and alderwood are ancient partners. This is the wood most favored by Native peoples of the Pacific Northwest for cooking salmon. While our method deviates slightly from the original, the effect of wood smoke on this most spectacular of fish remains true. Salmon simply seems to have been made for cooking this way. If you have a whole salmon, fillet and remove pin bones as shown, opposite.

1 alderwood plank, 12–16 inches long (or 2 planks set together)

1 side (about 3 lb) Pacific salmon, skin on but pin bones removed

sea salt and freshly ground pepper

2 small Vidalia onions, thinly sliced

3 cloves garlic, chopped

2 tbsp mustard seeds

2 green onions, finely chopped

2 tbsp chopped fresh rosemary

2 tbsp rice wine vinegar

2 tbsp olive oil

1 large lemon for squeezing

Preheat grill to high.

Season flesh side of salmon with sea salt and pepper. In mixing bowl, combine onion, garlic, mustard, green onion, rosemary, vinegar and olive oil. Stir to blend and season with salt and pepper to taste. Pat this mixture over flesh side of salmon pressing firmly to form a crust.

Season soaked plank with sea salt, place on grill, close lid and bake for 3 to 5 minutes or until it begins to crackle and smoke. Carefully open lid and gently lay side of salmon skin-side down on plank. Close lid and plank-bake for 12 to 15 minutes until cooked to medium doneness. Check occasionally to ensure plank is not on fire. Use spray bottle to extinguish any flames and close lid afterwards. Once salmon is done, squeeze lemon over entire length, remove from grill and transfer to serving platter. Serve with lemon wedges.

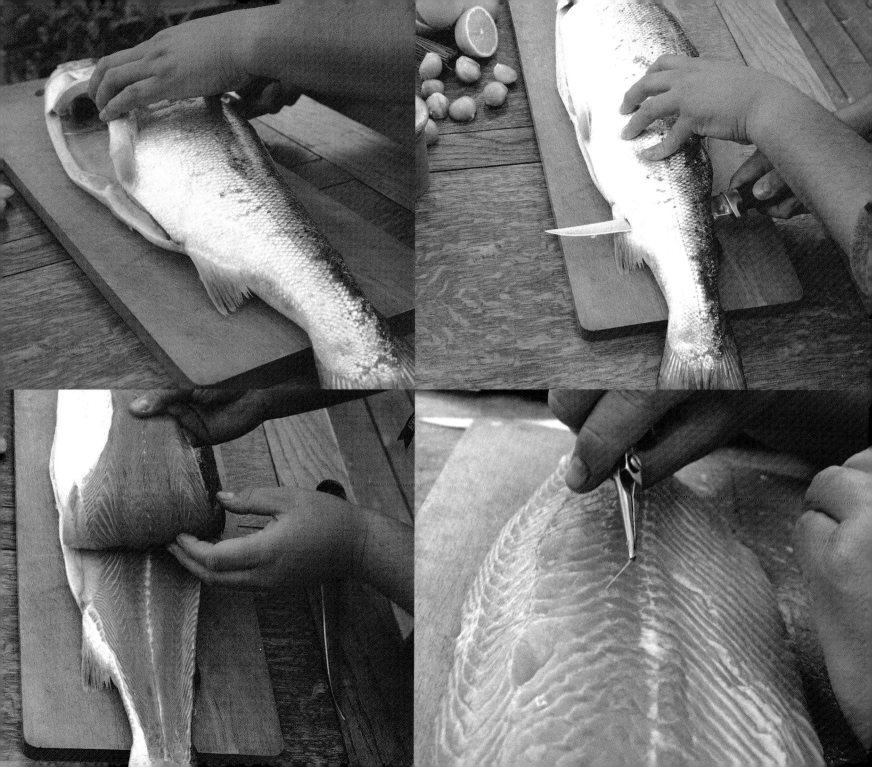

Cedar-Planked Arctic Char with Summer Savory and Partridge Berry Relish

Some cooks liken Arctic char to rainbow trout or salmon trout and, indeed, if you can't easily find Arctic char, these trout work well for this recipe. Choose fish that are no larger than a pound each.

SERVES 4 TO 6

2 cedar planks, soaked
4 whole fresh Arctic char (approximately 1 lb each)
1 large bunch summer savory
4 shallots, diced
1 tbsp cracked black pepper
1 oz Newfie Screech Dark Rum, or other dark rum
1 orange, halved and thinly sliced
8 tsp butter
sea salt and freshly ground pepper
Partridge Berry Relish (recipe follows)

Preheat grill to high.

Season Arctic char inside and out with sea salt and pepper. Pull off a few sprigs of summer savory and chop finely; reserve remainder. Combine chopped savory with shallots, black pepper and rum. Season with sea salt and mix together well. In cavity of each fish, place 3 orange slices, a quarter of the shallot mixture and 2 tsp butter.

Place soaked planks on grill, close lid and bake for 3 to 5 minutes until they begin to crackle and smoke. Carefully lift lid, place half of remaining summer savory on planks, and lay Arctic char over savory. Cover fish with remaining savory and close lid. Plank-bake for 15 to 18 minutes until fully cooked and tender. Serve with *Partridge Berry Relish*.

Partridge Berry Relish

MAKES APPROXIMATELY 2 CUPS

Partridge berries are indigenous to Newfoundland. Unless you live in that province, they may be difficult to obtain (although you may find them frozen in supermarkets or specialty food stores). Substitute cranberries, blackberries, blueberries or lingonberries or a combination.

2 cups Newfoundland partridge berries

3/4 cup white sugar

1 sprig fresh summer savory

1 tsp coarsely ground black pepper

1/4 tsp ground nutmeg

1/2 cinnamon stick

water as needed

In medium saucepan, combine berries with sugar, summer savory, black pepper, nutmeg, cinnamon and water to cover. Bring slowly to a rolling boil, reduce heat to low, cover and simmer for 15 minutes, stirring occasionally until thickened. Skim froth, if necessary, and let cool. Serve with *Cedar-Planked Arctic Char with Summer Savory*.

Planked Halibut Fillets with Green Onion Paste and Roasted Lemon Butter

Halibut lends itself well to the high heat used for planking. Its creamy white flesh and mellow flavor are immeasurably enhanced by smoke and spice – not to mention the fabulous Roasted Lemon Butter.

SERVES 6

2 hardwood planks, soaked
1 tbsp lemon pepper seasoning
3 cloves garlic, halved
6 green onions, chopped
2 tbsp roughly chopped fresh dill
1 tbsp mustard seed

1 tbsp dill seed
3 tbsp olive oil
sea salt
6 fresh halibut fillets (6 oz each)
Roasted Lemon Butter (recipe follows)

In food processor, combine lemon pepper, garlic, onions, dill, mustard seed, dill seed and olive oil and blend to a paste. Season with salt to taste. Rub this green onion paste well into fillets. Cover with plastic and let marinate, refrigerated, for 2 hours.

Preheat grill to high. Place soaked planks on grill, close lid and bake for 3 to 5 minutes or until they begin to crackle and smoke. Carefully open lid and place 3 seasoned halibut fillets on each plank. Close lid and plank-bake for 12 to 15 minutes until cooked to medium doneness. Remove from grill and serve with *Roasted Lemon Butter*.

Roasted Lemon Butter

1 cedar plank, soaked
4 lemons, halved
4 cloves garlic, halved
1/2 lb softened butter

1 tbsp chopped fresh dill
1 tbsp freshly ground black pepper
sea salt

MAKES APPROXIMATELY 1-1/2 CUPS

Preheat grill to high. Place soaked plank on grill, close lid and bake for 3 to 5 minutes or until it begins to crackle and smoke. Carefully lift lid and place lemon halves cut-side down on plank. Arrange garlic cloves around lemons and close lid. Plank-bake for 15 minutes until lemons are hot, soft and slightly charred.

Carefully remove lemons with tongs and, wearing oven mitts, squeeze lemons into bowl to collect all the juice. Reserve juice and let cool. Finely chop roasted garlic and add to lemon juice along with butter, dill and black pepper. Season with salt to taste.

Cover with plastic wrap (or shape into a log and wrap in waxed paper) and refrigerate until needed. The lemon butter will keep for up to 8 weeks in the freezer.

Granite-Roasted Pickerel with Lemon Pepper Ricotta Crust

Pickerel is the best choice for this recipe, but if you can't obtain it easily, choose striped bass or red snapper.   **SERVES 8**

<u>2 pieces granite</u>
<u>8 fresh pickerel fillets, skin on (6 oz each)</u>
<u>2 tbsp lemon pepper seasoning</u>
<u>1 cup firm ricotta</u>
<u>4 green onions, finely chopped</u>
<u>2 tbsp chopped fresh dill</u>
<u>juice of 1 lemon</u>
<u>2 tsp coarsely ground black pepper</u>
<u>sea salt</u>
<u>olive oil for brushing</u>
<u>fresh lemon wedges</u>

Preheat oven to 450°F. Place granite on middle shelf of oven and preheat for 15 minutes.

Meanwhile, season pickerel fillets with lemon pepper, rubbing it well into flesh. In mixing bowl, combine ricotta, green onion, dill, lemon juice and black pepper. Mix well and season with salt to taste. Use a portion of this mixture to form crust on flesh side of each pickerel fillet.

Brush surface of the granite with a little olive oil. Using metal spatula, transfer pickerel fillets to granite, skin-side down. Bake for 7 to 10 minutes until fish is opaque and crust is golden brown. Remove from oven and serve immediately with extra lemon wedges.

Cedar-Planked Atlantic Lobster Cakes with Curry Citrus Mayo

If you could taste affluence we think it would be pretty much like these outstanding little lobster cakes. Crab cakes, as good as they are, pale by comparison.

SERVES 8

2 cedar or applewood planks, soaked
1/2 cup homemade or quality store-bought mayonnaise
1 medium-size egg
1 clove garlic, chopped
2 tbsp fresh orange juice
1 tbsp chopped fresh coriander
2 green onions, thinly sliced
1/2 tsp ground cumin
1/2 tsp curry powder
1 tsp *Bone Dust Barbecue Spice* (page 15)
1-1/2 lb cooked Atlantic lobster meat (removed from shell)
    fresh, canned or frozen (drained)
sea salt and freshly ground pepper
hot sauce
1-1/2 cups coarsely ground wholewheat cracker crumbs
Curry Citrus Mayo (recipe follows)

Preheat grill to high.

In large mixing bowl, whisk together mayonnaise, egg, garlic, orange juice, coriander, green onion, cumin, curry and *Bone Dust*. Gently fold in cooked lobster meat and season to taste with salt, pepper and hot sauce. Add cracker crumbs and continue to mix gently, blending until mixture is loosely bound. Form into 8 small cakes. (Use an ice-cream scoop to make it easier.)

Place soaked planks on grill, close lid and bake for 3 to 5 minutes until they begin to crackle and smoke. Carefully open lid and, using metal spatula, transfer lobster cakes to hot planks. Close lid and plank-bake for 8 to 10 minutes. Check occasionally to ensure the wood is not burning and extinguish any flames with spray bottle. Remove cakes from planks with spatula and transfer to a serving platter. Serve with *Curry Citrus Mayo*.

Curry Citrus Mayo

1-1/2 cups homemade or quality store-bought mayonnaise
1 tsp coarsely ground black pepper
1 tsp curry powder
1 tsp orange zest, blanched, dried and finely chopped
1/4 cup fresh orange juice
1 tbsp chopped fresh coriander
sea salt

MAKES
1-3/4 CUPS

In medium bowl, whisk together mayonnaise, pepper, curry powder, orange zest and juice and coriander. Season to taste. Cover with plastic wrap and refrigerate for 1 to 2 hours to allow flavors to develop. Serve with *Cedar-Planked Atlantic Lobster Cakes*.

Pancetta-Wrapped Oysters on Chardonnay Vines with Roasted Garlic Sauce

SERVES 6

No matter what the season, if the month has an "r" in it, fire up the grill to make this elegant presentation. Make the Roasted Garlic Sauce *first. It will become your favorite barbecue sauce – it's great with everything from ribs to shrimp.*

6 Chardonnay-vine skewers, soaked in warm water for an hour
    (or wooden skewers soaked for an hour in Chardonnay)
24 fresh large oysters, shucked and drained
2 tbsp *Bone Dust Barbecue Spice* (page 15)
2 tbsp chopped fresh coriander
12 slices pancetta (Italian unsmoked bacon),
    partially cooked and drained of excess fat
sea salt and freshly ground pepper
1/2 cup *Roasted Garlic Sauce* (recipe follows)

Preheat grill to high.

In wide skillet, bring 3 cups water to a rolling boil. Blanch oysters in water for 1 minute. Remove with slotted spoon and plunge into ice water to stop cooking process. Drain and pat dry with paper towels.

Season oysters with *Bone Dust* and coriander. Cut each slice of partially cooked pancetta in half, widthwise. Tightly wrap each oyster in half a strip of pancetta. Skewer 4 pancetta-wrapped oysters on each vine or skewer. Grill oyster skewers for 8 to 10 minutes until oysters are firm and pancetta is crisp, basting liberally as they cook with *Roasted Garlic Sauce*. Serve immediately.

Roasted Garlic Sauce

1 small Vidalia onion (or other mild onion), sliced
2 tbsp olive oil
1/2 cup roasted garlic purée (see *Maple-Planked Brie*, page 24)
2 tbsp molasses
2 tbsp cider vinegar
2 tsp *Bone Dust Barbecue Spice* (page 15)
1 tbsp chopped fresh rosemary
1/2 cup light beef broth
1-1/2 cups quality store-bought barbecue sauce
sea salt and freshly ground pepper

MAKES APPROXIMATELY 2 CUPS

In medium saucepan over medium-high heat, sauté onion in olive oil for 2 to 3 minutes until transparent and tender. Add roasted garlic purée, molasses, cider vinegar, *Bone Dust*, rosemary, beef broth and barbecue sauce. Bring to boil, stirring occasionally. Reduce heat to low and let simmer for 15 minutes. Remove from heat and purée with hand blender (or in food processor or blender). Strain and let cool.

Pine-Needle-Smoked Mussels

Yes, there is another use for dry pine needles besides throwing them on the fire. This inventive recipe takes mussels to another level entirely. Make sure your grill is in an open, well-ventilated space – neither the middle of a forest nor an apartment balcony, for instance!

SERVES 4 TO 6

<u>Kitchen bucket of dry pine needles</u>
<u>3 lb fresh mussels, cleaned and debearded</u>
<u>3 tbsp coarse sea salt</u>
<u>1 bunch fresh rosemary, leaves removed from the stems</u>
<u>juice of 2 limes</u>
<u>freshly ground black pepper</u>

Preheat grill to high.

Season mussels with sea salt. In large mixing bowl, combine 3 or 4 handfuls of pine needles with rosemary. Mix well.

Place mussels directly on grill. Cover with pine needle–rosemary mixture, close lid and let mussels grill-roast for 4 to 5 minutes until they open. Be careful when opening the lid; there will be a lot of smoke and ash. Blow or fan off the remaining ash and discard any unopened mussels. Place mussels on a large serving platter, squeeze limes over them, season with black pepper and serve immediately with lots of warm crusty bread.

Planked Sea Bass with Cuban Mojito Sauce

A big, dense sea bass done up with a gently fiery Cuban-style sauce – delish! Make the Cuban Mojito Sauce *first, as you will need it for marinating.*

2 cedar planks, soaked
8 skinless fillets of sea bass (6 oz each, about 2 inches thick)
sea salt and freshly ground pepper
Cuban Mojito Sauce (recipe follows)
2 limes for squeezing

Season sea bass fillets with salt and pepper, place in dish and pour half of the *Cuban Mojito Sauce* over fish. Let marinate for 30 minutes.

Preheat grill to high. Season soaked planks with sea salt, place on grill, close lid and let bake for 3 to 5 minutes until they begin to crackle and smoke. Carefully open lid and place marinated fish fillets on planks. Close lid and plank-bake for 15 to 18 minutes, or until cooked to medium doneness. Check periodically to make sure plank is not on fire and use spray bottle to extinguish any flames. While sea bass is baking, heat remaining *Cuban Mojito Sauce*. Squeeze limes over sea bass. Carefully remove planks from grill and, using metal spatula, transfer sea bass to platter. Serve immediately with warm *Cuban Mojito Sauce*.

Cuban Mojito Sauce

Use rubber gloves when handling hot chiles and avoid contact with your face.

MAKES
APPROXIMATELY
1-1/2 CUPS

1/4 cup plus 2 tbsp vegetable oil
1 medium onion, diced
1–2 Scotch bonnet chiles, seeded and diced
2 roasted red peppers, peeled and seeded
2 tbsp chopped fresh coriander
2 bay leaves
1 cup tomato sauce
sea salt and freshly ground pepper

In medium saucepan, heat oil over medium-high heat. Sauté garlic, onion and chile peppers for 3 to 4 minutes until tender. Add roasted red peppers, coriander and bay leaves and continue to cook for 4 more minutes, stirring occasionally. Add tomato sauce. Bring mixture to a rolling boil, reduce heat and simmer for 15 minutes. Season with salt and pepper to taste. Remove and discard bay leaves. Purée mixture using hand blender (or in food processor or blender) until smooth and thick. Adjust seasoning and cool.

CHAPTER 4

From the Earth

SIDES AND SAUCES

Maple-Planked Roast Corn

Planked Fennel Salad
with Malt Vinaigrette

Stuffed Twice-Baked Smoked Potatoes

Cedar-Planked Vidalia Onion Barbecue Sauce

Terra-Cotta-Roasted Shallots and
Parsnips with Vanilla

Cedar-Roasted Garlic Aïoli

Oak-Roasted Tomato Cream Sauce

Plank-Roasted Root Vegetables

The vegetables, salads, savory condiments — such as the world's greatest aïoli — and an outstanding pasta sauce that comprise this chapter illustrate quite effectively just how versatile planking and stone-roasting can be. While we don't suggest soaking planks and firing up the grill just to make *Cedar-Planked Vidalia Onion Barbecue Sauce*, or *Oak-Roasted Tomato Cream Sauce*, you might prepare them when you are using the grill for other planking or traditional grilling recipes. Since planking emphasizes the natural sweetness inherent in many vegetables (such as corn, onions and root vegetables), you may want to team them alongside unplanked items from time to time. All of these recipes are versatile: both the *Terra-Cotta-Roasted Shallots and Parsnips with Vanilla* and the *Plank-Roasted Root Vegetables* work well with traditional roast beef, pork, chicken or lamb. The *Stuffed Twice-Baked Smoked Potatoes* can be successfully made the day before and reheated to sit alongside classic grilled flank steak or burgers.

Woods such as almond or pecan, if you can obtain them, are wonderful for planking. They add a sweet nuttiness to vegetables, aged cheeses and meats such as chicken, turkey and pork. Applewood enlivens the flavor of vegetables and seafood and actually darkens the skin of chicken to an attractively burnished color.

To pump up the flavor of vegetables further, place water-soaked citrus peel, cinnamon sticks, whole nutmegs, garlic cloves and any number of herbs with the vegetables on the plank. As the spices and herbs smolder and smoke, their flavors work their way into the food adding a whole other dimension.

Maple-Planked Roast Corn

Roasting corn over a hot grill is pretty basic – usually it involves plunking unshucked ears of corn right down on the grill. For planked corn, however, you remove the husk and silk and, after a presoaking, lay the stripped corn right on the plank. Stripping the corn makes it easier for the smoky flavors to penetrate.

SERVES 6

<u>1 maple plank, soaked</u>
<u>6 ears corn, shucked</u>
<u>1 tbsp *Bone Dust Barbecue Spice* (page 15)</u>
<u>butter</u>

Preheat grill to high. Soak ears of corn in cold water for 30 minutes. Remove corn from water, shake off excess water, then season with *Bone Dust*.

Place soaked plank on grill, close lid and bake for 3 to 5 minutes or until it begins to crackle and smoke. Carefully lift lid, lay ears of corn on hot plank and close lid. Plank-roast for 10 to 15 minutes turning corn occasionally. Check to make sure wood is not burning and use spray bottle to extinguish any flames. Reduce heat to medium if necessary. Remove corn from grill, roll in butter, season with a little additional *Bone Dust* if desired and serve immediately.

Planked Fennel Salad with Malt Vinaigrette

Two often-overlooked ingredients – fresh fennel and good old malt vinegar – combine here to produce an unusual but very good salad that makes a terrific accompaniment to seafood and fish entrées.

SERVES 6 TO 8

1 cedar plank, soaked
1 head fennel, trimmed and sliced
1 medium onion, sliced
salt and freshly ground pepper
1 green bell pepper, seeded and thinly sliced
4 ripe plum tomatoes, seeded and thinly sliced
1 tbsp chopped fresh sage
1/4 cup olive oil
3 tbsp malt vinegar
1 tsp white sugar
1 tbsp Dijon mustard
salt and freshly ground pepper

Preheat grill to high.

In mixing bowl, combine sliced fennel and onion and season with salt and pepper to taste. Place soaked plank on grill, close lid and bake for 3 to 5 minutes until it begins to crackle and smoke. Carefully lift lid, place fennel and onion mixture on plank, close lid and plank-roast for 10 to 15 minutes until vegetables are golden brown. Check occasionally to make sure wood is not burning. If necessary, use spray bottle to extinguish any flames and reduce heat to medium. Remove from grill and let cool.

Slice fennel into thin strips. In bowl, combine fennel, onion, green pepper, tomato, sage, oil, malt vinegar, sugar and Dijon mustard. Season with salt and pepper to taste and let sit for 30 minutes before serving.

Stuffed Twice-Baked Smoked Potatoes

Potato lovers will line up with their plates when they smell these humongous beauties smoking just out of the oven. Here is an example of oven-planking using a pre-soaked plank. These are to the world of potatoes what Mark McGwire homers are to baseball: out-of-the-park winners.

1 hickory plank, soaked

4 large baking potatoes, scrubbed

1 medium onion, sliced

4 cloves garlic, peeled

6 slices bacon, diced and cooked crisp

1/3 cup butter

1/4 cup sour cream

1-1/2 cups grated smoked Cheddar cheese (about 6 oz)

3 green onions, chopped

2 tsp *Bone Dust Barbecue Spice* (page 15)

salt and freshly ground pepper

Preheat oven to 450°F. Place soaked plank on baking sheet and set on middle rack of oven to bake for 10 minutes.

While plank is heating, slice potatoes in half lengthwise. Using sharp knife, diamond score cut side of potatoes; this will make it easier to scoop out flesh once potatoes are baked. Season with salt to taste. Place potatoes, cut side down, on hot plank. Lay sliced onion and garlic on top of potatoes. Bake for 1-1/2 hours or until potatoes are cooked and tender and onions and garlic are cooked and slightly charred. Remove from oven. Let cool for a few minutes, then finely chop onions and garlic and set to one side.

Carefully scoop flesh of potatoes out of skins and place in large bowl. Don't tear or break skin as this is the vehicle for the final stuffing. Mash flesh and add bacon, butter, sour cream, smoked Cheddar, green onions, *Bone Dust*, and charred onions and garlic. Season with salt and pepper to taste and mix thoroughly. Spoon potato mixture into the 8 potato skins, pressing firmly to stuff them really well. Return to oven (plank not necessary) and bake for 15 minutes or until heated through. Serve immediately with *Roll-in-the-Hay-Wrapped Steak with Herb and Pepper Butter* (page 46).

Cedar-Planked Vidalia Onion Barbecue Sauce

This amazingly good — and chunky — barbecue sauce is the essence of versatility: use it as a basting sauce or as a finishing sauce with grilled meats. We even like it stirred into homemade chilies or soups.

MAKES
APPROXIMATELY
4 CUPS

1 cedar plank, soaked
3 medium Vidalia onions, sliced
8 cloves garlic
2 tbsp *Bone Dust Barbecue Spice* (page 15)
1/4 cup olive oil, divided
1/2 cup bourbon, divided
1 cup hickory smoke–flavored barbecue sauce
1 cup rich beef broth
2 tbsp horseradish (preferably freshly grated)
1 tbsp chopped fresh rosemary
salt and freshly ground pepper

Preheat grill to high.

In bowl, toss onions and garlic together with *Bone Dust* and 2 tbsp olive oil. Place soaked plank on grill, close lid and bake for 3 to 5 minutes until it begins to crackle and smoke. Carefully lift lid, lay seasoned onion mixture on plank and close lid. Plank-roast for 15 to 20 minutes, turning onions occasionally, until slightly charred and tender. Remove from grill and let cool. Coarsely chop garlic.

In large saucepan, heat remaining olive oil and sauté onions and garlic for 3 to 5 minutes. Pour in 1/4 cup bourbon and scrape up any bits clinging to bottom of pan. Add barbecue sauce, beef broth, horseradish and rosemary. Bring to boil, reduce heat to medium-low and simmer, stirring occasionally, for 15 to 20 minutes. Add remaining bourbon and season with salt and pepper to taste. Remove from heat and cool. Use on ribs, steaks and chicken.

Terra-Cotta-Roasted Shallots and Parsnips with Vanilla

These vanilla-scented roasted roots are simply outstanding with roast beef and venison. You will need a large, relatively shallow earthenware casserole. If you're planning a roast pork (or, even better, the Cedar-Plank Roast Rack of Pork with Maple Tarragon Mustard Glaze, *page 39), add a couple of peeled apples or pears to the mix.*

SERVES 6 TO 8

12 shallots, peeled

4 parsnips, scraped, in diagonal 1/2-inch slices

3 tbsp olive oil

2 tbsp balsamic vinegar

2 fresh vanilla bean pods (make sure they are plump and soft)

salt and freshly ground pepper

2 tbsp chopped fresh parsley

Preheat oven to 425°F.

In bowl, combine shallots, parsnips, olive oil and balsamic vinegar. Using small, sharp knife, slice vanilla pods in half lengthwise and scrape out seeds. Add vanilla seeds and pods to bowl, toss together well and season with salt and pepper to taste.

Transfer vegetable mixture to terra-cotta casserole and place in oven to roast for 45 minutes or until golden brown and tender. Remove from oven, toss with parsley and serve.

Cedar-Roasted Garlic Aïoli

This decidedly contemporary rendition of a classic French preparation is wonderful with oven-roasted potato wedges or grilled fish. Use it as a dip for grilled shrimp or as the centerpiece for a platter of crudités.

MAKES APPROXIMATELY 2 CUPS

1 cedar plank, soaked
6 heads garlic
4 large egg yolks
1 tbsp Dijon mustard
2 tbsp red wine vinegar
1 cup extra virgin olive oil
1-2 dashes hot sauce
1-2 dashes Worcestershire sauce
1 tbsp chopped fresh thyme
1/4 cup freshly grated Parmesan cheese
salt and freshly ground pepper

Preheat grill to high.

Prepare garlic: Cut top off of each head and peel away as much excess skin as possible; leave heads and last layer of skin intact.

Place soaked plank on grill, close lid and bake for 3 to 5 minutes or until plank begins to crackle and smoke. Carefully lift lid, place heads of garlic on plank and plank-roast for 45 minutes or until garlic is soft and tender. Check from time to time to make sure plank is not burning. If necessary, use spray bottle to extinguish any flames and reduce heat to medium-high. When garlic is done, remove from plank and let cool.

Hold garlic heads upside down over mixing bowl and squeeze firmly to remove smoked cloves of garlic. Pick out any remaining cloves with a metal skewer. Add egg yolks, Dijon mustard and red wine vinegar to garlic cloves and whisk together. Once mixture is well combined, add olive oil in thin stream, whisking, until mixture is emulsified, smooth and creamy. Add hot sauce, Worcestershire sauce, thyme and grated cheese. Season with salt and pepper to taste and blend well. Transfer to small covered container and refrigerate until ready to use.

Oak-Roasted Tomato Cream Sauce

Use this robust, full-bodied sauce to dress pasta or to finish a risotto. It's equally good as a complement to fish, chicken or veal. Use a presoaked plank for this oven-roasted method.

MAKES
APPROXIMATELY
8 CUPS

2 oak or other hardwood planks, soaked
16 ripe plum tomatoes, halved lengthwise
salt and freshly ground pepper
8 cloves garlic, peeled
1 medium onion, sliced
3 tbsp olive oil
2 tbsp tomato paste
1 cup tomato juice
1 cup chicken broth
4 sprigs basil
1 tbsp crushed dried chiles
1 cup heavy cream

Preheat oven to 425°F. Place soaked planks on baking sheet and bake on middle rack of oven for 10 minutes.

In the meantime, season tomatoes with salt and pepper to taste. When planks are hot, lay tomatoes, cut-side down, on planks. Place cloves of garlic and sliced onions on top of tomatoes. Add 1 to 2 cups of water to baking sheet to keep planks from smoking too much. Plank-roast tomatoes for 50 to 60 minutes or until tomatoes are slightly charred and tender and onions and garlic are soft. Remove from oven.

Heat olive oil in large saucepan over medium-high heat and sauté roasted garlic and onions for 3 to 5 minutes. Add tomato paste and stir. Add roasted tomatoes, tomato juice, chicken broth, basil and chiles. Give everything a good stir and bring to boil. Reduce heat to medium-low and simmer, stirring occasionally, for 45 minutes. Purée with hand blender (or in food processor or blender) and return to saucepan. Season with salt and pepper to taste. Add cream, bring to a gentle boil and cook for another 10 minutes. Remove from heat and let cool.

Plank-Roasted Root Vegetables

Oven-roasted potatoes and other root vegetables are all the rage in restaurants and with home chefs, but simple oven-roasting doesn't provide the unmistakably good smokiness and depth of flavor produced by plank-roasting.

SERVES 8

1 cedar plank
1 small butternut squash, peeled and seeded
2 large carrots, scraped
2 large parsnips, scraped
1 small celery root, peeled
1 large onion, peeled and cut into 12 wedges
12 cloves garlic
2 tbsp coarsely ground black pepper
1/4 cup malt vinegar
3 tbsp vegetable oil
salt and freshly grated nutmeg
water, apple cider or juice as needed

Preheat oven to 425°F.

Cut squash, carrots, parsnips and celery root into 2-inch chunks. In large bowl, toss together onions, garlic, squash, carrots, parsnips, celery root, pepper, vinegar and oil. Season liberally with salt and nutmeg.

Place plank in roasting pan large enough to hold it loosely and add enough water, cider or juice to float plank. Place pan with plank in oven to heat for 10 minutes. Place vegetables on plank and roast for 45 to 60 minutes or until vegetables are tender and slightly charred. Season again if necessary and serve.

CHAPTER 5

From the Orchard

SWEETS AND TREATS

Bourbon and Honey–Planked Pears
with Mascarpone Fool

Maple-Planked Bourbon-Soaked Peach Melba
with Warm Summer Berries and Sour Cream Ice

Terra-Cotta-Baked Apples
with Cinnamon Ice Cream

Vine-Skewered Toasted Marshmallow
S'more Cheesecakes

Planked Cheddar Biscuits

Fresh, ripe, succulent peaches, crisp apples and pears, exotic mangoes — these and many other fresh fruits traditionally provide the perfect ending to grilled fare. It may seem improbable, but these fruits are even more magnificent when paired with some of the planking techniques we've outlined in this book.

When fruit is warmed over any heat source, the flesh caramelizes slightly as natural sugars rise to the surface helping to almost self-glaze the peach, pear or apple. Add to this the unmistakable aroma and flavor of plank smoke and you've got the beginning of a truly sweet ending.

In a number of the following preparations you'll find recipes within recipes: for example, *Maple-Planked Bourbon-Soaked Peach Melba with Warm Summer Berries and Sour Cream Ice* or our take on a classic winter dessert, *Terra-Cotta-Baked Apples with Cinnamon Ice Cream*. These delightful preparations are sufficiently versatile to be enjoyed on their own or in tandem with other desserts.

And remember, although some of these recipes may sound detailed and lavish, they are quite easy to pull together and will make a grand impression on family and friends. Try the *Vine-Skewered Toasted Marshmallow S'more Cheesecakes* and see what we mean!

Bourbon and Honey–Planked Pears with Mascarpone Fool

This is a stunning presentation to offer at the end of a formal fall dinner. The small russet-toned Seckel pears are a good choice for this dish. Their firm flesh and slightly spicy flavor can stand up to and will be immeasurably enhanced by a proper planking!

SERVES 8

1 cedar plank, soaked
3/4 cup bourbon
1/2 cup honey
freshly ground black pepper
freshly grated nutmeg

8 small ripe pears
1 tbsp fresh lemon juice
Mascarpone Fool (recipe follows)
8 sprigs fresh mint

In small saucepan over medium-high heat, combine bourbon and honey. Season with pepper and nutmeg. Bring to boil, reduce heat and simmer until liquid is reduced by half. Remove from heat and cool. Set to one side.

Thinly slice pears part-way through from bottom towards top, keeping stem intact, but cutting far enough up so as to be able to spread them out like a fan. Arrange sliced pears in dish just large enough to hold them in one layer and brush with lemon juice. Spoon 1 tbsp bourbon-honey mixture over each pear and let marinate for 1 hour.

Prepare *Mascarpone Fool* and chill.

Preheat grill to high. Place soaked plank on grill, close lid and bake for 3 to 5 minutes or until it begins to crackle and smoke. Carefully lift lid, place pears on plank and close lid. Plank-bake for 10 to 12 minutes or until pears are hot and tender. Remove pears from plank and transfer to dessert plates. Garnish each pear with a dollop of *Mascarpone Fool*, drizzle with remaining bourbon-honey mixture, add a sprig of mint and serve immediately.

Mascarpone Fool

1/2 cup whipping cream
1 cup mascarpone cheese

1 tsp pure vanilla extract
2 tsp white sugar

MAKES APPROXIMATELY 2 CUPS

In small chilled bowl, whip cream until stiff. In separate bowl, mix mascarpone, vanilla and sugar. Gently fold in whipped cream. Cover and refrigerate until serving time. Serve with *Bourbon and Honey–Planked Pears*.

Maple-Planked Bourbon-Soaked Peach Melba with Warm Summer Berries and Sour Cream Ice

Somewhere in the world this dessert would probably be deemed against the law – it's that good. It is actually three desserts in one: the Maple-Planked Bourbon Peaches, *the* Warm Summer Berries, *and the* Sour Cream Ice. *All three are quite wonderful on their own but in concert with each other, they're gangbusters.*

SERVES 4

2 maple planks, soaked
orange juice as needed
8 ripe peaches, halved and pitted
1/4 cup pure maple syrup
freshly ground black pepper
8 scoops *Sour Cream Ice* (recipe follows)
   or quality vanilla ice cream
Warm Summer Berries (recipe follows)
4 sprigs fresh mint

Preheat oven to 425°F. Place soaked planks in roasting pan or ovenproof dish (use 2 if necessary) and pour in enough orange juice to come up to top edge of planks. Place in oven and preheat for 15 minutes or until wood is hot.

Place peaches cut-side down on planks and bake in oven for 20 minutes or until cooked and warmed through. Remove from oven and let cool slightly. Using small, sharp knife, carefully peel peaches. Slice each

peach half into 8 pieces and transfer to mixing bowl. Add maple syrup and black pepper to peaches and toss gently.

To serve, place 2 scoops of ice cream in each dessert dish. Spoon a quarter of the warm peach mixture over ice cream and top with *Warm Summer Berries*. Garnish each serving with a sprig of fresh mint.

Warm Summer Berries

These berries are also lovely on their own or with thick cream or custard.   **SERVES 8 TO 12**

1-1/2 cups fresh red currants

3 cups fresh raspberries

1-1/2 cups fresh blueberries

1-1/2 cups fresh (or frozen) sour
    cherries, pitted

1-1/2 cups fresh strawberries, sliced

2 cups red wine

2 cups cranberry juice

1 cinnamon stick, broken in half

1/2 cup white sugar

juice and zest of 1 orange

1-1/2 tbsp tapioca

Place fruit in colander and sort through, discarding any that is spoiled. Transfer one-quarter of the fruit to food processor or blender and purée.

In saucepan, combine purée with red wine, cranberry juice, cinnamon stick, sugar and orange juice and zest. Bring to boil, reduce heat and simmer for 15 minutes. Add tapioca and boil until thick. Strain purée through sieve set over bowl, gently stirring and pressing against sides of sieve to collect all the strained purée you can. Pour hot purée over remaining fresh berries and gently fold together. Serve with *Maple-Planked Bourbon-Soaked Peaches*.

Sour Cream Ice

1 cup water

1/2 cup white sugar

1 tsp pure vanilla extract

1 tbsp fresh lemon juice

3 cups sour cream (not low-fat)

2 egg whites, lightly beaten

1/4 cup honey

MAKES APPROXIMATELY 4 CUPS

In saucepan, combine water, sugar, vanilla and lemon juice. Bring to boil and simmer for 5 minutes. Remove from heat and cool completely.

In large mixing bowl, whisk together sour cream, sugar-water mixture, egg whites and honey until smooth. Pour into ice-cream maker and freeze according to manufacturer's instructions. Transfer to a suitable container and freeze. Serve with *Maple-Planked Bourbon-Soaked Peaches*.

Terra-Cotta-Baked Apples with Cinnamon Ice Cream

Big bountiful apples stuffed with raisins, walnuts, spices and brown sugar and served with home-made Cinnamon Ice Cream – stupendous! We also love these fragrant apples with warm custard.

SERVES 4

4 large baking apples
1/2 cup brown sugar
1/4 cup sultanas or golden raisins
1/2 cup chopped walnuts

1 tsp cinnamon
1/4 tsp ground ginger
1 cup plus 2 tbsp apple cider
Cinnamon Ice Cream (recipe follows)

Preheat oven to 350°F.

Core apples, leaving half an inch at the base of each apple.

In mixing bowl, combine brown sugar, raisins, walnuts, cinnamon, ginger and 2 tbsp apple cider and mix together well. Fill the apples with this mixture.

Place apples in terra-cotta baking dish, pour in 1 cup apple cider, and bake for 40 to 45 minutes or until apples are soft. Remove from oven. Serve with *Cinnamon Ice Cream* (recipe follows).

Cinnamon Ice Cream

1 cup whipping cream
1 cup whole milk
1 cinnamon stick
1 tsp pure vanilla extract

6 large egg yolks
2/3 cup white sugar
1 tsp cinnamon

MAKES APPROXIMATELY 4 CUPS

In saucepan, over moderately high heat, combine cream, milk, cinnamon stick and vanilla. Allow mixture to scald, heating it just below boiling. Meanwhile, in bowl, whisk together eggs, sugar and cinnamon until just blended. Continue whisking as you slowly pour scalded milk into egg mixture. Pour very slowly so that eggs warm gradually and don't scramble.

Return custard mixture to saucepan and cook over medium-high heat, stirring with wooden spoon constantly to keep mixture from sticking to base of saucepan. Do not allow it to boil. Cook for approximately 5 to 6 minutes until mixture thickens and coats the back of spoon. Strain custard through sieve into large bowl and let cool. Freeze in ice-cream maker according to manufacturer's instructions. Transfer to a suitable container and freeze. Serve with *Terra-Cotta-Baked Apples*.

Vine Skewered Toasted Marshmallow S'more Cheesecakes

The kids' favorite campfire sweet upgraded to become suitable for adults – finally! Enjoy with or without kids. Use a 12-cup muffin tin with cups large enough to accommodate a trimmed graham wafer.

SERVES 8 TO 12

2 vine skewers or wooden skewers, soaked for 1 hour
12 graham wafers
1 lb cream cheese, softened (2 8-oz packages)
2 large eggs
1 tsp fresh lemon juice
1/2 tsp pure vanilla extract
1/2 cup white sugar
30 large marshmallows
3 tbsp all-purpose flour
1-1/2 cups milk chocolate chips
chocolate sauce (purchased or homemade), warmed

Lightly butter and flour muffin tin. Tap out excess flour. Trim square edges of graham wafers with a sharp knife to make them round. Place in muffin tin.

Preheat grill to high and oven to 350°F.

In large mixing bowl, combine cream cheese, eggs, lemon juice, vanilla and sugar. Beat with electric mixer until smooth, about 4 to 5 minutes. Set to one side.

Skewer marshmallows onto vines or wooden skewers. Toast over hot grill (or open fire) until golden brown and soft. Transfer to microwave-safe bowl and microwave on high for 20 seconds to soften completely. Fold softened marshmallows into cream cheese mixture, combining thoroughly.

Spoon batter into graham wafer–lined muffin cups, filling each about 3/4 full. Place 1 tbsp chocolate chips into center of each cake and swirl in with a toothpick. Place in preheated oven and bake for 25 to 30 minutes until golden brown and a tester inserted in the middle of a cake emerges clean. Remove from oven and let cool for about 20 minutes. When completely cool, run a knife around edge of each cake to loosen and gently invert onto tray. To serve, drizzle cakes with a little warm chocolate sauce.

Planked Cheddar Biscuits

MAKES 12
BISCUITS

Wood-smoked Cheddar biscuits warm from the oven – wow! Serve them with homemade chilies and soups, or spread them with apple butter or apple jelly and serve with pork.

1 hickory plank, soaked
2 cups all-purpose flour
3 tsp baking powder
1 tsp salt
1/3 cup butter
2 tsp coarsely ground black pepper
1 tbsp chopped fresh sage
1/2 cup grated old Cheddar cheese
2/3–3/4 cup milk
melted butter for brushing

Preheat oven to 450°F. Place soaked plank in oven to preheat for 10 minutes.

In mixing bowl, sift together flour, baking powder and salt. Using pastry blender, cut butter into flour until mixture is the consistency of coarse meal. Add black pepper, sage and cheese. Mix gently. Add milk gradually, mixing lightly until dough forms a ball that separates from sides of bowl. (You may not need all the milk.) Turn biscuit dough onto floured work surface, knead gently for 30 seconds, and then roll or pat out to a thickness of 3/4 inch. Cut out biscuits with floured cutter.

Using metal spatula, transfer biscuits to hot plank and bake for 12 to 15 minutes or until biscuits are golden brown and puffed up nicely. Brush with melted butter while still warm and serve.

Ted Reader wishes to thank:

Steven Mintz of Uni Foods, thank you for all your support and encouragement;
your guidance and faith in my skills has been very important to me

Mark Lindros of P&H Foods, Butterball, thank you for the turkeys

Adam Kennedy of Heritage Salmon, thank you for the salmon

Jim Vidoczy of Ontario Pork, thank you for the pork

Sylvia Bielak of Lazar Gourmet Foods, thank you for the beef

Danny Soberano of All Seas Fisheries, thank you for the cedar planks and seafood

Louis and Larry of Nikolaou Restaurant Equipment, thank you for your kindness

Theresa Stahl of Weber Grills, thank you for the wonderful barbecue

Jim Beam Bourbon, you're the tastiest

Dave Nichol, thank you for the great beer (Dave's Scotch Ale and Dave's Honey Brown Lager)
used in two of the recipes and quite often before, during and after testing

Lourie Silvera (Chef Luther's father-in-law), thank you for the hay used in the Roll-in-the-Hay-Wrapped Steak

Michael Olson, chef of On the Twenty Restaurant and Cave Spring Cellars, thank you
for all of the grapevines and for your creative encouragement

Olaf Mertens, chef and colleague of the Boneyard Bar-B-Que Restaurant, thank you
for your recipe ideas and friendship

Dale McCarthy, chef of the Delta Meadowvale Resort and Conference Center, thanks for
letting Luther work with me on Cottage Country and on the testing of these recipes

Cottage Country Television, thank you Craig, Adele and all of the gang for your support and
exceptional work. It has been a blast

Thank you to all of my friends at the Loblaws and the President's Choice Test Kitchen for
embracing my planked salmon recipe. You promoted this recipe with passion and it gives me
great pleasure to see cedar planks being sold in your grocery stores

And to all my friends and colleagues who helped taste and test the recipes in this book.

Index

A

Aïoli, roasted garlic, 80
Alderwood planks, salmon with onion and
    mustard crust on, 56
Ale, and Cheddar cheese soup, 16
Apples, baked, 90
Applewood planks,
    stuffed pork tenderloin on, 42
Arctic char with summer savory and
    partridge berry relish, 60

B

Bacon:
    and wheat berry salad, 31
    wrapped beef tenderloin with blue
        cheese cobbler, 38
Balsamic raspberry glaze, 48
Banana leaves, grouper wrapped in, 54
Barbecue sauce, Vidalia onion, 78
Barbecue spice, bone dust, 15
Barley and smoked-bacon salad, 31
Beef:
    prime rib with beer and mustard, 37
    steaks,
        sirloin, 40
        strip loin, 46
    tenderloin with blue cheese cobbler, 38
Beer:
    and hay-wrapped steaks, 46
    prime rib roast with mustard and, 37
Berries, warm summer, 89
Biscuits, Cheddar cheese, 93
Blue cheese cobbler, 38
Bonavista tartar sauce, 29
Bone dust barbecue spice, 15
Bourbon-soaked peach Melba, 88
Bread and wild rice stuffing, 36

Brie with roasted garlic and peppers, 24
Burgers, lamb, 49
Burgundy vines, beef skewers with
    onions and mushrooms, 40
Butters:
    chipotle chile lime, 55
    herb and pepper, 46
    roasted lemon, 62

C

Cedar planks:
    Arctic char with summer savory and
        partridge berry relish, 60
    bourbon and honey pears with
        mascarpone fool, 86
    chicken with herbs and Cheddar
        cheese, 45
    chicken thighs, honey garlic, 35
    crown rack of lamb with savory
        stuffing, 44
    fennel salad with malt vinaigrette, 75
    lobster cakes with curry citrus
        mayo, 64
    onion and portobello mushroom
        focaccia, 26
    rack of pork loin with maple tarragon
        mustard glaze, 39
    risotto with Taleggio and peas, 27
    roasted garlic aïoli, 80
    roasted root vegetables, 83
    roasted shallot and shiitake
        polenta, 19
    salmon fillets with shallot and
        dill crust, 53
    sea bass with Cuban mojito sauce, 70
    turkey with wild rice and bread
        stuffing, 36
    Vidalia onion barbecue sauce, 78
Chardonnay-vine skewers:

pancetta-wrapped oysters on, 66
    shrimp and pineapple with chile
        lime rub, 23
Cheddar cheese:
    biscuits, 93
    and brown ale soup, 16
    chicken with herbs and, 45
Cheese, prosciutto-wrapped figs
    stuffed with, 18
Cheesecakes, marshmallow, 92
Chicken:
    breasts, with smoky corn salsa, 34
    with herbs and Cheddar cheese, 45
    thighs, honey garlic, 35
Chipotle chile lime butter, 55
Chowder, corn, 17
Cider glaze, 43
Cinnamon ice cream, 90
Cinnamon sticks, quail on, 30
Clams, and mussels roasted, 22
Cobbler, blue cheese, 38
Cod, Newfoundland cakes, 28
Corn:
    chicken with, 34
    chowder with sausage, 17
    roasted, 74
Cornbread, and sweet potato stuffing, 43
Cornmeal, shallot and shiitake
    polenta, 19
Cuban mojito sauce, 71
Cumin-roasted pearl onions, 15
Curry citrus mayo, 65

D

Dill butter sauce, 22

F

Fennel salad with malt vinaigrette, 75
Figs, prosciutto-wrapped, stuffed

with cheese, 18
Focaccia, onion and portobello
    mushroom, 26
Fool, mascarpone, 86

G

Garlic. See Roasted garlic
Glaze:
    balsamic raspberry, 48
    cider, 43
    maple tarragon mustard, 39
Goat cheese onion slaw, 49
Granite:
    lamb burgers, 49
    Newfoundland cod cakes, 28
    pickerel with lemon pepper
        ricotta crust, 63
    prosciutto-wrapped figs stuffed
        with cheese, 18
Grouper wrapped in banana leaves, 54

H

Halibut with green onion paste and
    roasted lemon butter, 62
Hay-wrapped steak with herb and
    pepper butter, 46
Herb and pepper butter, 46
Hickory planks:
    beef tenderloin with blue cheese
        cobbler on, 38
    Cheddar biscuits, 93
    chicken with smoky corn salsa, 34
    corn chowder with sausage, 17
    twice-baked potatoes, 76

I

Ice, sour cream, 89
Ice cream, cinnamon, 90

L

Lamb:
   burgers, 49
   crown rack of, 44
Leaves, about, 10
Lemon butter, 62
Lemon pepper ricotta crust, 63
Lobster cakes with curry citrus mayo, 64

M

Maple planks:
   bourbon-soaked peach Melba, 88
   brie with roasted garlic and peppers, 24
   Cheddar and brown ale soup, 16
   prime rib roast with beer and mustard, 37
   roast corn, 74
Maple tarragon mustard glaze, 39
Marshmallow cheesecakes, 92
Mascarpone fool, 86
Mayonnaise:
   aïoli, 80
   curry citrus, 65
Mesquite planks:
   chicken with smoky corn salsa, 34
   corn chowder with sausage, 17
Mushrooms:
   portobello focaccia, 26
   shiitake, and shallot polenta, 19
Mussels:
   and clams roasted, 22
   pine-needle smoked, 68

N

Newfoundland cod cakes, 28

O

Oak planks:
   chicken thighs, honey garlic, 35
   scallops, 52
   tomato cream sauce, 82

venison strip loin, 48
Onion and portobello mushroom focaccia, 26
Onions, barbecue sauce, 78
Oysters, pancetta-wrapped on skewers, 66

P

Parsnips and shallots with vanilla, 79
Partridge berry relish, 61
Peach Melba, 88
Pearl onions, cumin-roasted, 15
Pears, bourbon and honey-planked, 86
Pickerel with lemon pepper ricotta crust, 63
Pine needles, smoked mussels, 68
Pistachio-crusted scallops, 52
Pizza with onion, bacon and gorgonzola, 20
Planks, about, 7-8
Polenta, shallot and shiitake, 19
Pork:
   rack of, with maple tarragon mustard
      glaze, 39
   tenderloin, stuffed, 42
Potatoes, twice-baked, 76
Prime rib roast with beer and mustard, 37
Prosciutto-wrapped figs stuffed with
   cheese, 18

Q

Quail on cinnamon sticks, 30
Quinoa and smoked-bacon salad, 31

R

Raspberry, balsamic glaze, 48
Relish, partridge berry, 61
Rice, risotto with Taleggio and peas, 27
Ricotta, lemon pepper crust, 63
Riesling dill butter sauce, 22
Risotto, with Taleggio and peas, 27
Roasted garlic aïoli, 80
Roasted garlic sauce, 67
Roasted lemon butter, 62

S

Salad, wheat berry and bacon, 31
Salmon:
   how to fillet, 57
   with shallot and dill crust, 53
   with Vidalia onion and mustard crust, 56
Salsa, corn, 34
Sauces:
   Cuban mojito, 71
   Riesling dill butter, 22
   roasted garlic, 67
   tartar, 29
   tomato cream, 82
   Vidalia onion barbecue, 78
Sausage, corn chowder with, 17
Savory stuffing, 44
Scallops, pistachio-crusted, 52
Shallots, and parsnips with vanilla, 79
Shrimp, on vine skewers, 23
Skewers:
   beef sirloin on, 40
   pancetta-wrapped oysters on, 66
   shrimp and pineapple, 23
Slaw, goat cheese onion, 49
Smoke, about, 7
Soup:
   butternut squash, 14
   Cheddar cheese and brown ale, 16
Sour cream ice, 89
Squash, soup, 14
Starters:
   brie with roasted garlic and peppers, 24
   onion and portobello focaccia, 26
   pizza with onion, bacon and gorgonzola, 20
   prosciutto-wrapped figs stuffed
      with cheese, 18
   risotto with Taleggio and peas, 27
   roasted mussels and clams, 22
   shallot and shiitake polenta, 19
   skewered shrimp, 23

Stones, about, 8
Stuffing:
   cornbread and sweet potato, 43
   savory, 44
   wild rice and bread, 36
Sweet potato and cornbread stuffing, 43

T

Taleggio cheese, garlic risotto with
   peas and, 27
Tartar sauce, 29
Terra-cotta:
   baked apples, 90
   pizza with onion, bacon and gorgonzola, 20
   roasted mussels and clams, 22
   shallots and parsnips with vanilla, 79
Tomato cream sauce, 82
Turkey with wild rice and bread stuffing, 36

V

Vanilla bean pods, shallots and
   parsnips with, 79
Vegetables, roasted root, 83
Venison, strip loin with balsamic
   raspberry glaze, 48
Vines, about, 10
Vine skewers:
   beef sirloin, 40
   pancetta-wrapped oysters on, 66
   shrimp and pineapple, 23
   toasted marshmallow cheesecakes, 92

W

Warm summer berries, 89
Wheat berry and smoked-bacon salad, 31
Wild rice, and bread stuffing, 36
Wood-smoked butternut squash soup, 14

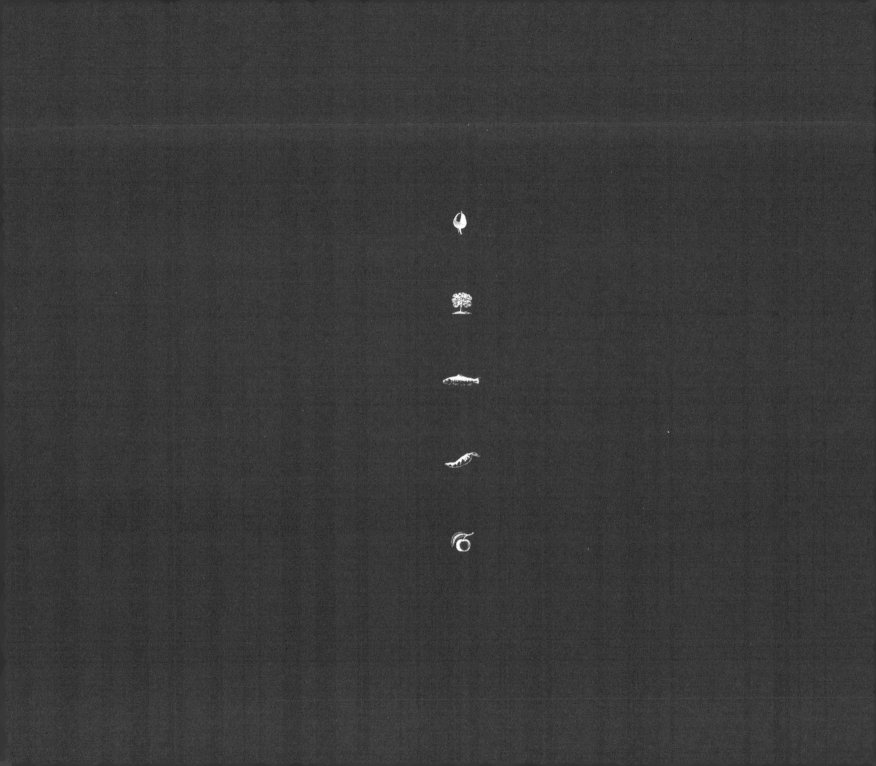